Successful Online Learning with Gifted Students

This innovative, technology-based resource provides those who teach gifted and advanced learners in grades 5–8 with quality, research-based, online lessons, tools, and insights.

Throughout, you'll find ready-to-implement virtual lessons, simulations, and learning modules. You'll also learn how to create, differentiate, and modify existing lessons through an online platform. In addition, the book offers helpful strategies addressing online student accountability, etiquette, and collaboration, and shares useful tips for communicating with parents.

Whether you are looking to enrich learning within the classroom, provide students with extensions outside the classroom, or engage students in distance learning, this book will be invaluable in meeting the needs of your gifted and advanced learners.

Vicki Phelps, Ed.D. is an Assistant Professor of Education at Milligan University where she teaches both undergraduate and graduate level courses. She has been involved in gifted education for over 20 years, including collaboratively developing and opening a gifted magnet school, providing professional learning opportunities to schools seeking to improve best practice in gifted education and differentiation, and writing gifted curricula. Dr. Phelps is the recipient of the 2021 NAGC Book of the Year Award (with Emily Mofield) for their coauthored work, *Collaboration, Coteaching, and Coaching in Gifted Education.*

Successful Online Learning with Gifted Students

Designing Online and Blended Lessons for Gifted and Advanced Learners in Grades 5–8

Vicki Phelps, Ed.D.

Routledge
Taylor & Francis Group

NEW YORK AND LONDON

Cover image: Shutterstock, ID: 626375054

First published 2022
by Routledge
605 Third Avenue, New York, NY 10158

and by Routledge
2 Park Square, Milton Park, Abingdon, Oxon, OX14 4RN

Routledge is an imprint of the Taylor & Francis Group, an informa business

© 2022 Taylor & Francis

Library of Congress Cataloguing-in-Publication Data
Names: Phelps, Vicki, author.
Title: Successful online learning with gifted students: designing online and blended lessons for gifted and advanced learners in grades 5-8 / Vicki Phelps.
Description: New York, NY: Routledge, 2022. | Includes bibliographical references and index.
Identifiers: LCCN 2021030894 | ISBN 9781032145112 (hardback) | ISBN 9781646322213 (paperback) | ISBN 9781003238317 (ebook)
Subjects: LCSH: Gifted children--Education (Elementary) | Gifted children--Education (Middle school) | Computer-assisted instruction--Curricula--Planning. | Blended learning.
Classification: LCC LC3993.22.P44 2022 | DDC 371.95--dc23
LC record available at https://lccn.loc.gov/2021030894
Access the Support Material: www.routledge.com/9781646322213

ISBN: 978-1-032-14511-2 (hbk)
ISBN: 978-1-646-32221-3 (pbk)
ISBN: 978-1-003-23831-7 (ebk)

DOI: 10.4324/9781003238317

Typeset in Palatino, Futura, and Rockwell
by MPS Limited, Dehradun

Access the Support Material: www.routledge.com/9781646322213

Dedication

To my loving husband, David, who endlessly encourages me to chase all my dreams,

To my children, Brittany, Becca, and David, whose love and support mean everything to me,

To my family, near and far, who inspire me and remind me of what is truly important in life.

Soli deo gloria.

● Contents

List of Figures

List of Tables

■ List of Support Material

As you read this book, you'll notice the Support Material icon next to the following tools. The icon indicates that these tools are available as protected downloads on our website, www.routledge.com/9781646322213, via the Instructor Hub so you can easily print and distribute them to your students.

Simulation links in Chapters 4 and 5 can all be found at www.routledge.com/9781646322213 via the Instructor Hub.

■ About the Author

Vicki Phelps, Ed.D. is an Assistant Professor of Education at Milligan University where she teaches both undergraduate and graduate level courses. She has been involved in gifted education for over 20 years, including collaboratively developing and opening a gifted magnet school, providing professional learning opportunities to schools seeking to improve best practice in gifted education and differentiation, and writing gifted curricula. She has authored work in *The New Teacher's Guide to Overcoming Common Challenges* and research publications related to gifted motivation, as well as co-authored (with Emily Mofield) the 2021 NAGC Book of the Year, *Collaboration, Coteaching, and Coaching in Gifted Education.* Vicki has enjoyed being a keynote speaker and an invited speaker at various conferences, and she thoroughly enjoys sharing her research, curricula, and teaching experiences at international, national, and state-level conferences.

Acknowledgments

This book never would have been possible without the support of people who provided me with not only a strong foundation of learning, but also with the support and belief that I could share my ideas with others. To Dr. Sally Thomson, Dr. Elizabeth Wilkins, Dr. Emily Mofield, and Kayren Craighead, thank you for believing in me and keeping me green and growing. To my editors for seeing the potential in my ideas and supporting me through developing this project into a reality. To all my students, each and every one, who have inspired me beyond words and helped me grow, not only as an educator, but also as a person.

Introduction

While technology is often synonymous with computers, technology has actually been an integral part of education stemming back to the early days before computers were even a mainstay in our daily lives. It's somewhat comical to imagine a time when the pencil was once on the cutting edge of technology. Needless to say, times have changed, and with the COVID-19 pandemic, technology became an even greater necessity in education as school systems relied heavily on current innovations to reach and teach through distance learning. Because of this, students were inundated with online tasks, and in some cases, online learning was negatively associated with a highly stressful time in their lives.

Over the course of the pandemic, disengagement and underachievement of gifted and advanced learners continued to grow as the focus became less on meeting the individual needs of students and more on teaching to the masses through an often-unfamiliar delivery model. In fact, for many learners, the lack of online access made opportunities for academic growth seem almost impossible. How then, can we as educators, continue to re-ignite our students' motivation and passion for learning to not only actively participate in online learning opportunities, but also to truly engage and persevere to go deeper into their learning?

This book was written with this question in mind. This book is *not* meant to simply be another text about the latest tech tools and online applications, but rather, this book is meant to serve as a guide for how to better meet the needs of gifted and advanced learners through the purposeful and innovative use of technology in online and blended classrooms. The goal is to provide a launching point to help educators better evaluate and integrate innovative instructional practice through technology to meet the needs of gifted and advanced learners, either as a differentiation tool within the classroom, as a form of enrichment beyond classroom learning, or as the venue for engaging and challenging lessons. In addition, this book recognizes the role of the teacher in online learning as someone who provides a presence, maintains continuity and guidance, motivates, and assists gifted and advanced learners in seeking help in areas of uncertainty (Ng & Nicholas, 2007).

For the purposes of this book, online learning is considered any learning that encourages the integration of technology as a means to guide student learning through the teaching process (Stein et al., 2011). Online learning is multifaceted (Vandenhoyten et al., 2014), and as such, it can be integrated through a variety of instructional models:

- **Enrichment Model:** Through enrichment, online learning is integrated into a traditional classroom as a means to "enrich" the learning experience for gifted and advanced learners. While this could be used in a multitude of ways, it might be part of curriculum compacting based on student readiness levels or as an enrichment tier during a Response to Intervention designated time.
- **Blended Model:** Blended learning, for the context of this book, recognizes the blending of instructional modalities (i.e., face-to-face, online) and instructional

DOI: 10.4324/9781003238317-101

methods (Graham, 2006). Blended learning can be achieved through purposeful and consistent integration of technology within a full-time "brick and mortar" classroom or through a hybrid model of instruction (see below).

♦ **Hybrid Model:** Hybrid learning, as referenced in this text, refers to a combination of face-to-face instruction in conjunction with distance learning (see below). As referenced above, hybrid learning is a form of blended instruction, as it recognizes the combination of delivery methods (Mortera-Gutierez, 2006).

♦ **Distance Model:** Distance learning refers to learning and instruction that takes place when an instructor and learners do not have a face-to-face classroom setting, necessitating fully dedicated online instruction (Rahman et al., 2015).

The "Why" Behind Technology

As educators, we should always be asking "why" we teach what we teach. What is the purpose behind each lesson, and "why" is that purpose relevant? If the overall goal is to present all students with new opportunities in learning, then what are we doing for our gifted and advanced learners who already know the material or are able to master it quickly (DuFour & DuFour, 2012)? How can technology serve as an additional tool to help us continue to reframe our instructional design to better meet their unique and complex needs? How can we best enrich, organize, communicate, and integrate technology to help gifted and advanced learners to shine (Stargardter, n.d.)?

You might be able to relate to the different trends and popular online options that have come to the forefront of online teaching over the past few years (e.g., Bitmoji classrooms, Google Forms assessments, Kahoots). While many of these trends can be powerful tools for online instruction, there is also the danger of implementing them without taking the time to ask the "why" behind their use as best practice. For example, there are some Bitmoji classrooms that look amazing, filled with beautifully decorated walls, awesome furniture, and all sorts of bells and whistles that students can click-on to provide a little extra humor or fun fact. All of this serves as a great hook to gain students' attention, but unfortunately, some Bitmoji classrooms stop there and do not include the same level of engaging learning opportunities for gifted and advanced learners. It does absolutely no good to put effort into creating an online learning task that does not provide students with opportunities to think deeply and critically about the topic of study. Likewise, it is meaningless to find a ready-made online resource for the sake of having "an online resource" if it does not engage students and move them forward in their learning.

As you begin to read the various chapters in this book, take the time to think about where your students are and how you can better meet their academic and affective needs. Take the time to evaluate which technology resources and applications will motivate your students for sustained engagement in learning. Keep the focus on implementing technology to enhance the learning process through deeper inquiry and innovative instructional practice, not just as a means to add a little more novelty. Ask the "why" and be purposeful.

Organization of the Book

Chapter 1 explores technology as a driving force in learning. Background information on gifted motivation and engagement, as well as underachievement in online learning, is also provided. Guidance for evaluating online learning tasks is explored, and an introduction to the "What, How, Why: Then Justify" approach is discussed as a foundation to online instructional design. Further features of differentiation, formative assessments, and reflection in online instruction complete the chapter.

Chapter 2 discusses the importance of collaboration and social interaction in online learning while also providing the context for understanding the role of task-valuation and individual interests. A variety of activities for establishing a conducive learning environment, creating a sense of community, and setting the stage for respectful and accountable talk within online instruction is also explored.

Chapter 3 introduces Google Forms as a tool for creating learning modules focused on meeting the needs of gifted and advanced learners. After a brief overview of the navigational features and key considerations of Google Forms, guidance on transforming existing lessons into learning modules and developing escape rooms and simulations is provided. The chapter concludes with a focus on providing personalized feedback.

Chapter 4 expounds upon and provides access to a fully developed Google Forms simulation guiding students through ACES Astronaut Training (Advanced Criteria Evaluation Specialists), which includes learning modules focused on advanced thinking processes. Through the context of the simulation, students are presented with a variety of research-based gifted processing tools to direct them into deeper analysis of content. In addition to providing access to this ready-to-implement simulation, step-by-step directions are provided for how to create an online simulation in this manner.

Chapter 5 provides an overview of how to implement a long-term simulation through Google Sites. After an overview of key features, the chapter establishes the purpose, structure, and guiding principles for integrating gamification into this type of simulation experience, focused on eliciting greater motivation and engagement from gifted and advanced learners. Classroom management tips and instructions for implementing the ready-to-use homesite are also provided.

Chapter 6 shares examples of additional applications for continued engagement and enrichment through virtual field trips, choice boards, virtual showcases, and various other options to enrich online instruction. The I-LEARN Process for independent study is introduced as a guiding structure for online independent research, along with multiple strategies to further engage gifted and advanced learners in online learning.

Chapter 7 delves into supporting parents and guardians as partners in online learning by focusing on key areas of identified need and proactive planning. Structures for successful home learning are discussed, and then the conclusion and final thoughts are shared.

How to Use This Book

This book is not meant to be, nor is it, a book strictly focused on the latest and most innovative technology tools. This book's ultimate goal is to serve as a thinking tool to build capacity on how to better meet the unique learning needs of gifted and advanced learners through online and blended learning. As you read through the book, remain mindful that gifted educators are developers of talent who have the opportunity to evaluate, implement, and utilize technology as a means to motivate and engage students to demonstrate their gifts and natural abilities through talents and competencies (Gagné, 2008).

In order to best meet the goal of seeking out and developing the talents of all learners, we must also remain mindful of students who are culturally, linguistically, and economically diverse. Even more importantly, before we can move forward with online instruction, we have to first recognize and address how we can continue to not only meet the needs of diverse and underserved populations, but also offer equal opportunities to students who might not have online access outside of the classroom due to geographic location, socioeconomic status, or any other circumstance.

As online instructional practice continues to impact these opportunities for growth, planning for online instruction *must also include* accommodations and modifications to equalize and normalize the opportunity for continued engagement and growth in learning for all students. We must recognize that gifted and advanced learners need daily challenge, the opportunity to work independently, socialization with like-ability peers, and a differentiated pace in instruction (Swan et al., 2015). This is possible. This is achievable. This simply requires maintaining the same level of rigor and creativity within instruction, while modifying how the assignment is to be accessed and completed. As you utilize this book, remain mindful of how the same design principles for online instruction can be incorporated through more traditional means.

Chapter 1

Technology as a Driving Force in Learning

In today's changing times, the classroom is constantly evolving. As such, learning takes place through traditional learning scenarios within a brick and mortar classroom, as well as through online enrichment, blended classroom learning, and distance learning. Regardless of the approach, technology is a valuable tool to better meet the needs of gifted and advanced learners, and without question, there are a multitude of online resources available. The predominant problem is that very few online resources are appropriately created to meet the unique learning needs of gifted and advanced learners.

Gifted and advanced learners require more than just advanced content and fast pacing. They also need opportunities to delve deeper into content, process information in complex ways, creatively problem-solve, and connect abstract concepts to higher levels of critical thinking (VanTassel-Baska, 2009). Hence, it becomes even more important to search for online sites and resources that are founded in gifted pedagogy, while also learning how to create and incorporate best practice in designing and implementing new lessons within your own instructional practice.

Gifted Motivation and Engagement

Before moving into the realm of curricular design for online and blended learning, it is important to understand which approaches and types of learning motivate and engage gifted and advanced learners. First and foremost, at a foundational level, motivation is a prerequisite for higher levels of student engagement (Saeed & Zyngier, 2012) and leads students to persist and engage with tasks, coursework, and future endeavors over extended periods of time (Wigfield et al., 2004). Motivation is key during online and blended learning (Webinar, 2020). Therefore, if key motivational factors for gifted and advanced learners can

DOI: 10.4324/9781003238317-1

be identified, then curricula can be designed and modified to encourage these heightened levels of engagement. Unfortunately, this is often a challenge in distance learning scenarios.

Primarily, it has been found that gifted and advanced learners are most motivated by an integration of autonomous learning which supports active involvement in the learning process (i.e., Fakolade & Adeniyi, 2010; Kahyaoglu, 2013; Patrick et al., 2015; Phelps, in press; Webinar, 2020). This is in contrast to the commonly found online activities of 'drill and kill' assignments which continue to teach students through high levels of repetition and very little real-world application or focus on individual interests and values. In fact, when gifted and advanced students are able to pursue learning through areas of individual interest and personal value systems, their motivation, engagement, and levels of achievement are increased (Fakolade & Adeniyi, 2010). In addition, personal input, choice, critical thinking, and increased levels of challenge further increase these heightened levels of motivation (Gentry & Springer, 2002; Powers, 2008). Each of these attributes becomes a key guiding factor as online learning continues to impact instructional practice.

While autonomous learning is consistently linked to increased motivation in gifted and advanced learners, it is also important to recognize how students are able to become actively involved in the learning process. Within the context of integrating technology into the learning process, online learning is considered to be highly interactive and immersive for gifted and advanced learners (Donally, 2019; Huang et al., 2019; Siegle, 2019). Additional instructional methods which incorporate these high levels of active learning include online simulations, experiments, constructions, independent study, and debate, just to name a few.

Underachievement in Online Learning

All too often, however, the unique learning needs of gifted and advanced learners are not addressed in the online learning environment, leading to underachievement and disengagement with the learning process. When examining the role of underachievement in gifted learners, both psychosocial (e.g., goal setting, task management, perseverance, etc.) and educational features of gifted pedagogy need to be explored. These needs can be further explained through The Four Pillars of Tertiary Student Engagement and Success (Ronksley-Pavia & Neumann, 2020):

- ◆ Behavioral engagement: attendance, participation, presence
- ◆ Affective engagement: attitude, interest and enjoyment
- ◆ Social engagement: sense of belonging with learning environment, connections with peers and teachers, involvement
- ◆ Cognitive engagement: self-regulation, setting goals, mastery focused learning

Each of these factors play a large role in continuing to meet both the psychosocial and advanced academic needs for this population.

Furthermore, Neihart and Betts' (2020) six gifted profiles (see Table 1.1) also examine how to address disengagement and underachievement in gifted learners. By integrating the

Table 1.1 Guiding Principles for the Design of Online Learning for Gifted and Advanced Learners

Gifted Learner Profiles [1]	Guiding Principles for Online Instructional Design
The Historically Underserved Learner (adapted from At-Risk Learner): The historically underserved learner might feel rejected or defensive and often does not receive the appropriate supports to nurture their gifts and talents. Their interests often lie outside of school-focused curriculum.	♦ Create a safe and structured online learning environment that embraces diversity. ♦ Design personalized online learning plans focused on student interests and value-systems (e.g., independent study, differentiated learning modules, etc.). See Chapters 2 and 6. ♦ Provide consistent and ongoing positive, purposeful, and constructive feedback. ♦ Provide frequent check-ins and integrate short-term goals.
Autonomous Learner: Autonomous learners have recognized how to navigate the educational system to create new opportunities for themselves. They typically have positive self-concepts, are successful, and receive positive attention. Autonomous learners are self-directed, independent, and communicate effectively.	♦ Provide freedom in learning through access to diverse, stimulating, and flexible online learning spaces and applications. ♦ Encourage engagement through collaborative online learning experiences. See Chapter 6. ♦ Foster continued motivation for ongoing, extended online learning opportunities through consistent, purposeful, and constructive feedback. ♦ Incorporate opportunities for online independent study in areas of interest. See Chapter 6. ♦ Provide online opportunities, tools, and applications to inspire, extend, and facilitate student growth.
Creative Learner: The creative learner has strong divergent skills and may appear to be stubborn or sarcastic. They frequently question authority and do not conform to norms. Despite having a strong sense of humor that appeals to their peers, they typically suffer from low self-esteem.	♦ Integrate online collaborative opportunities that encourage interpersonal skills. See Chapter 2. ♦ Allow flexibility in online learning to allow for students to express themselves creatively (e.g., choice boards, collaborative community building, etc.). See Chapters 2 and 6. ♦ Incorporate values and student self-awareness into online reflections of learning.

(Continued)

Table 1.1 (Continued)

Gifted Learner Profiles [1]	Guiding Principles for Online Instructional Design
	◆ Seek out online mentors to encourage a positive role-model for creative growth. ◆ Encourage personal goal setting in online learning.
Successful Learner: Successful learners account for up to 90% of identified gifted learners. They know how to successfully navigate the system and score highly on assessments. They rarely exhibit undesired behaviors, yet frequently choose to get by with as little effort as possible. They seem to have lost both creativity and autonomy due to failing to embrace the necessary skills for life-long learning.	◆ Provide opportunities for online autonomous learning and student choice (e.g., choice boards, independent study, gamification, etc.). See Chapter 6. ◆ Provide opportunities for leadership within collaborative online learning tasks and community building activities. See Chapter 2. ◆ Encourage online reflections of learning focused on intrinsic motivation and valuation of learning vs seeking attention on performance and external praise. ◆ Provide ongoing opportunities for appropriately challenging online learning tasks that require academic and psychosocial risk-taking.
Twice-Exceptional Learner: The twice-exceptional learner has one or more additional exceptionalities in conjunction with giftedness. Twice-exceptional learners are often overlooked for gifted identification and struggle with their abilities to perform in school. While often impatient and critical, stress might manifest through frustrations, helplessness, and isolation.	◆ Focus on a strength-based approach to online learning. ◆ Encourage online reflections that encompass self-awareness in regard to perseverance and valuation of student voice in learning. ◆ Provide consistent, purposeful, and constructive feedback that is focused on clear recognition of student gifts. ◆ Reduce risks of distractions during online learning by providing clear structure and expectations of online learning. ◆ Incorporate frequent check-ins during online learning to support students' success in achieving short-term and long-term goals.

(Continued)

Table 1.1 (Continued)

Gifted Learner Profiles [1]	Guiding Principles for Online Instructional Design
Underground Learner: Underground learners, typically females, deny their talents in order to 'fit in' with their non-gifted peers. They are usually anxious, insecure, and in conflict with meeting expectations from teachers and parents.	♦ Model being a life-long learner. ♦ Encourage student voice and provide regular reassurance through consistent, purposeful, and constructive feedback. ♦ Value independence through the integration of autonomous online learning tasks (e.g., independent study, choice boards, simulations, etc.). See Chapters 4 through 6.

[1] (Neihart & Betts, 2020).
Note. Adapted from Ronksley-Pavia and Neumann, 2020.

Four Pillars of Tertiary Student Engagement and Success (Ronksley-Pavia & Neumann, 2020) with the six gifted profiles, Table 1.1 provides suggestions for how to address underachievement and disengagement in gifted and advanced learners through purposeful design and implementation of online and blended learning.

Evaluating Online Learning Tasks

Ultimately, as online resources are sought out and/or developed, an awareness of keeping the learning fresh and new for gifted and advanced learners needs to be at the forefront. This not only continues to build curiosity within the learning process (Swan et al., 2015), it also creates a learning venue that is ready to embrace authentic learning experiences. In doing so, learning tasks are focused on active engagement and personal connection to the advanced skills, content, and real-world applications. Table 1.2 provides an overview of guiding criteria to consider while evaluating and designing online learning tasks. In addition, Resource 1 provides a pre-planning guide for designing online learning for gifted and advanced learners.

Table 1.2 Guiding Criteria for Evaluating Online Learning for Gifted and Advanced Learners

Which online learning resources are most supportive of the following questions?	
Key Criteria Focus	**Guiding Questions for Evaluation**
Advanced Content:	◆ Which advanced content standards are being addressed through this online learning task? ◆ How is the advanced content supported by the NAGC Gifted Programming Standards (NAGC, 2019)? ◆ How is advanced vocabulary integrated into the learning process? ◆ How is the ceiling 'lifted' for assessing the advanced level of learning? ◆ How does the online learning task provide opportunities to think as a disciplinarian in the field?
Active Student Involvement	◆ How is the student involved in the learning process (e.g., simulations, experiments, constructions, etc.)? ◆ How does the online learning task allow the student to demonstrate levels of understanding *beyond* selecting correct 'answers' (e.g., multiple choice, matching, etc.)? ◆ How is the student challenged to think through different perspectives or recognize how they are a personal stakeholder in the content?
Autonomous Learning Attributes:	◆ How does the learning reflect student interest? ◆ In what ways is student choice integrated into the learning objectives? ◆ How does the online learning task support students' task valuation (see Chapter 2)? ◆ How are students able to contribute personal insights and input into the online learning tasks?
Complexity	◆ How does the online learning task integrate multiple variables into learning (e.g., change over time, cross-curricular connections, perspectives, patterns, etc.)? ◆ How are constraints (e.g., limited word count, integration of specific components, time, etc.) utilized as a means to increase level of difficulty?
Creativity	◆ How does the online learning task allow for students to create originality through new approaches, theories, adaptations, or versions related to the desired outcomes?

(Continued)

Table 1.2 (Continued)

Which online learning resources are most supportive of the following questions?	
Key Criteria Focus	**Guiding Questions for Evaluation**
	♦ In what ways are opportunities to express creativity through the arts integrated into the online learning task? ♦ How are the dimensions of creative thinking (Guilford, 1986) incorporated into the online task (e.g., flexibility, fluency, originality, elaboration)?
Depth	♦ How does this site encourage thinking as a disciplinarian? For example, *How would an environmental engineer utilize biomimicry in solving a global issue?* ♦ How might debate be integrated into the online topic as means to delve deeper into learning? ♦ How might the online learning task be brought into an online discussion to explore unanswered questions, details, trends in data, and additional insights to the topic?
Ability to Provide Feedback	♦ How does the online learning task have a method/avenue to provide meaningful online feedback (see section below)? ♦ How timely and accessible is the ability to provide student feedback throughout the online learning process? ♦ Is there an avenue for students to respond to or seek clarification from the provided feedback?
Psychosocial Skills	♦ How does the online option incorporate student re-flection into the learning process (see end of chapter)? ♦ How is the student encouraged to develop time management, goal-setting, and positive responses to set-backs throughout the learning process? ♦ What collaborative opportunities are available with this online learning option?
Real-World Connections	♦ In what ways does the online learning task help the student relate learning to their own life? ♦ In what ways are the learning targets connected to our global world?

Resource 1 Pre-Planning Guide: Designing Online Learning for Gifted and Advanced Learners

FocusArea	Pre-Planning Guide
	How might you incorporate the following into online lesson design?
Advanced Content	Learning Standards:
	Advanced Vocabulary Terms:
	Opportunities to think as a disciplinarian:
Active Student Involvement	Student Involvement (e.g., simulations, experiments, constructions, etc.):
	Guiding/Essential Question(s):
	Opportunities for integrating student perspectives and connections to content:
Autonomous Learning Attributes	Opportunities for student choice and integration of student interest:
Complexity	Integration of multiple variables:
	Integration of constraints:
Creativity	Opportunities for FFOE (Fluency, Flexibility, Originality, Elaboration):
	Opportunities for arts integration:
Depth	Online discussions (e.g., unanswered questions, trends in data, depth of details, personal insights, etc.):
Ability to Provide Feedback	Ease and accessibility for ongoing, purposeful feedback:
Psychosocial Skills	Integration of student reflection:
	Opportunities for goal setting, time-management, self-regulation:
	Collaborative learning opportunities:
Real-World Connections	Integration of real-world connections:

Foundations of Online Learning for Gifted and Advanced Learners

Regardless of the setting, technology becomes a powerful differentiation tool. As with any meaningful differentiation, pre-assessing student learning should always be the first step in planning to better meet the learning needs of *all* students. Whether this is accomplished through students completing concept maps (either hardcopy or online) to demonstrate all they know about a topic of study (see Figure 4.3 in Chapter 4), responding to a few well-developed questions prior to engaging in a unit of study, or taking a pre-test on content, the data gathered from pre-assessments continue to guide and inform the next steps of differentiated practice (e.g., tiered assignments, curriculum compacting, independent study, flexible grouping, etc.).

Defining the Learning Environment

Understanding the type of learning environment is an important factor in navigating how technology can best be used as a differentiation tool. Whether learning is taking place within a traditional brick and mortar classroom, as an extension of classroom learning, or through fully-dedicated distance learning, there are slight nuances and modifications that can be made in designing online and blended learning to best meet the needs of gifted and advanced learners.

While teaching within a traditional classroom setting, for example, technology becomes a powerful tool to engage gifted and advanced learners who require curriculum compacting because they have already mastered the current unit of study. Instead of having the students engage in computer programs that just *keep them busy*, this is a prime opportunity to engage students in learning that not only engages them, but also provides them with opportunities to extend their own levels of learning. The subsequent chapters of this book will provide suggestions for online learning tasks that could be used to better meet the needs of these students.

Technology is also a powerful differentiation tool for a traditional or blended classroom as a means to *extend* classroom learning. How many times have you found yourself wishing that you had 'more time' to take your students deeper in their learning? How many times have your students approached you about wanting to learn more about the topic you are studying, but you have had to tell them there is not enough time? With technology (and a little creativity) the opportunity for students to participate and interact with structured learning as an extension of the school day is a viable option. To be clear, this does not mean to inundate students with loads of homework. This approach to differentiation extends learning when students have a drive and thirst to go deeper into their learning. While any of the common online teaching tools can be used to encourage and engage students in continued learning opportunities outside of the classroom, Chapter 5 will specifically address how this can be planned, incorporated alongside classroom learning, and managed effectively through Google Sites.

There are also learning environments that are fully dedicated to online, distance learning. Whether a student and their family elect to participate in full-time online schooling or, due to extenuating circumstances, when distance learning is the only option, planning for distance learning presents yet another opportunity to ensure that gifted and advanced learners are provided with curricula that meet their advanced learning needs.

Without question, there is no shortage of online videos, games, tutorials, and lesson plans, but unfortunately, many of these are geared toward meeting the needs of the masses vs. creating learning experiences that are both engaging and challenging for gifted and advanced learners. This becomes even more prevalent in distance learning, as personal interactions are often not as consistent and timely as working with students in a traditional classroom setting where formative assessments are more readily available to guide instruction, sometimes on a moment-to-moment basis. Likewise, the feedback, redirection, and differentiation in traditional classrooms also help to reinforce learning and further establish clear expectations. How then, can these practices be better implemented through a distance learning framework? It can be as easy as What, How, Why: Then Justify!

What, How, Why: Then Justify!

As we continue to evaluate readily available online learning tasks or as we begin to develop our own online curricula, there are key components to keep the academic needs of gifted and advanced learners at the forefront of our instructional design. Based on VanTassel-Baska's (2009) Integrated Curriculum Model (ICM), this instructional strategy builds upon the need for gifted and advanced learners to be presented with advanced content, be given opportunities to engage with content through advanced thinking processes, and integrate advanced conceptual understandings as part of the learning process. Figure 1.1 provides a visual of how these different components work together to support the unique learning needs of gifted and advanced learners.

The goal of What, How, Why: Then Justify is to guide students to the 'magic in the middle' of this strategy: *Justify*. This magic happens when gifted and advanced learners are not only engaging with advanced content, thinking through advanced processes, and making connections to abstract concepts, but they are also actively engaged with *justifying* and explaining their synthesis of learning. Without having students explicitly justify the integration of these guiding principles, the risk is that the components could be completed without the needed integration of all three components. For instance, if a student was tasked with reading an advanced text and asked to answer questions through an advanced processing model (e.g., Paul and Elder's (2019) Elements of Reasoning, Kaplan's (2009) Depth and Complexity Thinking Tools, etc.), without reasoning through and explaining the connections that are made through abstract generalizations, the student would not be engaging with the advanced content in a manner that best meets their gifted needs. To better support the integration of these three guiding principles, a more detailed description follows.

Figure 1.1 What, How, Why: Then Justify.

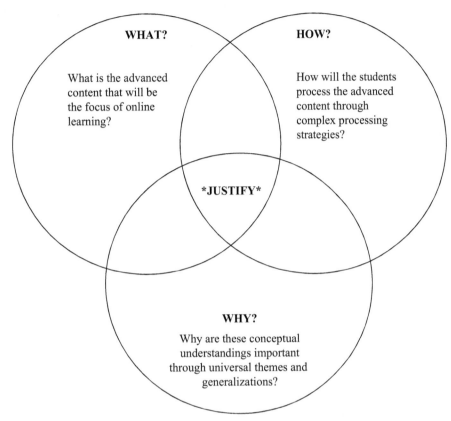

Note. Adapted from VanTassel-Baska, 2009.

The 'What'

When designing an online curriculum to challenge and engage gifted and advanced learners, begin by asking, *WHAT will the advanced content focus be for this particular online learning task?* The following questions are helpful in planning for this stage of curricular design.

- ◆ Which advanced standards will be addressed?
- ◆ What advanced materials (e.g., texts, problem-sets, vocabulary, etc.) will need to be uploaded or created?
- ◆ How might student interest and choice be integrated into this advanced content?
- ◆ How might cross-curricular connections be made through this topic of study?
- ◆ How might features of depth and complexity be integrated with this advanced content area?

The 'How'

When addressing how students will process the designated content, take the time to consider which gifted processing tools and strategies work best for the desired online learning task outcomes. When working with gifted and advanced learners, in particular, consider using advanced processing tools such as:

- **Depth and Complexity Thinking Tools** (Kaplan, 2009): Provides thinking tools to guide students to think about content as disciplinarians (e.g., language of the discipline, trends, change over time, multiple points of view, parallels, origins, etc.)
- **Elements of Reasoning** (Paul & Elder, 2019): Designed to encourage students' critical thinking skills of analyzing, evaluating, and improving one's thinking. Students use reasoning and evaluation to examine an issue or problem through a focused question, purpose, point of view, assumptions, concepts/big ideas, information/evidence, inferences/interpretations, and implications/consequences of a specified area of content.
- **Analysis Wheels** (Mofield & Stambaugh, 2016): Provides a framework to see the interconnectedness of content by recognizing how different relationships of content impact various other elements (e.g., how a setting influences conflict, how language influences tone, how structure impacts point of view, etc.).
- **Forecasting Model** (Juntune, 2013): Examines the causes/influences and effects/implications to a problem or issue, leading to further analysis of causes of causes and effects of effects, etc.
- **Six Thinking Hats** (de Bono, 2016): Encourages critical thinking through different perspectives of content: facts, feelings, cautions, benefits, processes, and creativity. Through exploring content through different perspectives, a greater depth of conceptual understanding is developed.

Whether one of these advanced processing tools is integrated into online learning or another strategy is chosen (e.g., inductive reasoning, concept-attainment, metaphorical reasoning, etc.), gifted and advanced learners need opportunities to analyze information and think critically about units of study. As such, when designing online learning experiences for gifted and advanced learners, consider the following questions to further guide curriculum development:

- In knowing Kaplan's Depth and Complexity Tools, in what ways might two or more of the thinking tools be integrated into guiding questions or incorporated into student responses in connection with the content?
- How might assumptions about a topic of study impact the implications stemming from a content specific problem? (Elements of Reasoning)
- In what ways does the setting of a text impact the identified conflict? (Literary Analysis Wheel)
- How can both positive and negative implications arise from a focused problem? What further effects stem from those implications? (Forecasting Model)
- How does the chosen topic impact which perspectives are most prevalent? (Six Thinking Hats)

The 'Why'

Once we have chosen advanced content and integrated advanced processing strategies into the design of online learning tasks, the next consideration is how to integrate universal themes (e.g., change, order vs. chaos, exploration, power, systems, etc.) and generalizations (e.g., change generates additional change, change can be either negative or positive, change is inevitable, etc.). A comprehensive list of universal themes and generalizations can be found at:

♦ http://emcsdgate.weebly.com/uploads/1/1/6/0/11600328/themes_generalizati ons.pdf

By integrating the universal themes and generalizations, gifted and advanced learners are given the opportunity to think abstractly and make connections to the global world.

When moving forward with integrating universal themes and generalizations, it is often helpful to focus on one theme throughout an entire unit of study or course of a year. In doing so, gifted and advanced learners are able to see how generalizations are applied across the context of different lessons and content areas. The following guiding questions provide examples of how to address the 'why' in the design of online learning.

♦ How might students create new generalizations tied to a specific theme and area of content?
♦ How might students connect specific content to universal themes and generalizations (e.g., create a spectrum, select *most* applicable, select *least* applicable, etc.).
♦ How might primary and secondary sources be utilized for students to create generalizations about a particular time period? How might those generalizations be further connected to universal themes and generalizations?

The 'Justify'

Having students justify their thinking is the 'magic in the middle' of the What, How, Why: Then Justify adaptation of the Integrated Curriculum Model (VanTassel-Baska, 2009). Clearly, gifted and advanced learners benefit from the integration of advanced content, advanced thinking processes, and connections to abstract thinking through universal themes and generalizations. This final component of *justify* provides gifted and advanced learners with the opportunity to articulate (e.g., orally, in writing, as part of a culminating project, etc.) their deeper levels of critical thinking of *how* and *why* they have made the analysis, decisions, and conclusions throughout the assigned learning task. Consider helping students in this endeavor by directing them to be specific in their justifications. This might be by asking: *Justify how your processing tools support your connection to the chosen universal theme and generalization(s).*

Resource 2 provides a guiding template for planning through the What, How, Why: Then Justify approach, helping to ensure that all areas are developed. Once these different foundational attributes of lesson design are addressed, then differentiation strategies for online learning can be appropriately implemented.

Resource 2 'What, How, Why: Then Justify' Planning Template

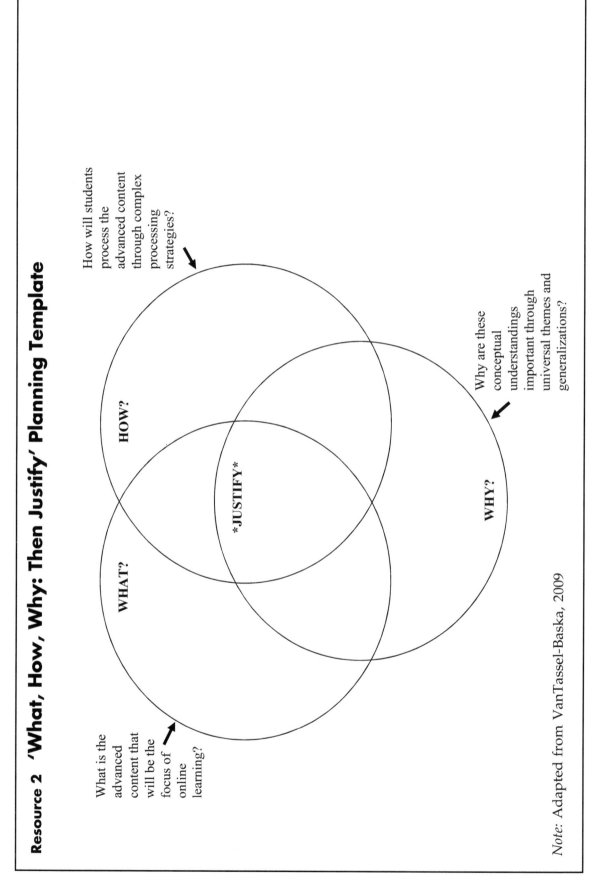

How will students process the advanced content through complex processing strategies?

HOW?

WHAT?

JUSTIFY

WHY?

Why are these conceptual understandings important through universal themes and generalizations?

What is the advanced content that will be the focus of online learning?

Note: Adapted from VanTassel-Baska, 2009

Copyright material from Phelps (2022), *Successful Online Learning with Gifted Students*, Routledge

Differentiation through Online Learning

With the pandemic of 2020, many teachers began to embrace distance learning through online meeting spaces (e.g., Zoom, Teams, etc.), and various learning management systems (e.g., Google Classroom, Canvas, Blackboard, etc.). While most educators are now much more familiar with creating an online meeting space, sending out the appropriate invites, and learning how to navigate the different features of screen sharing, chat boxes, breakout rooms, and integrating different backgrounds, the nuances of differentiating instruction for gifted and advanced learners continues to remain a challenge.

Pre-assessing for Online Learning

As with any classroom differentiation, the first step is to assess students' readiness levels through pre-assessment strategies. By learning what students already know about a topic of study, better informed decisions can be made on how to best meet students' individual needs throughout a unit of study. Table 1.3 provides a variety of methods to pre-assess student readiness levels prior to a unit of study. From this pre-assessment data, flexible grouping and differentiated instruction can then be used to better meet students' academic needs based on their levels of readiness.

Once placed in flexible groups, online meeting spaces can be better utilized to provide all students with the appropriate levels of challenge. While this management of learning can easily be done by an individual teacher, online learning also offers an opportunity for collaborative co-teaching through online meeting spaces. In particular, Friend and Cook's (2017) Station Teaching, referred to as Carrousel Teaching in the gifted context (Mofield & Phelps, 2020), provides students with an opportunity to rotate through different stations of learning that incorporate vertical differentiation (Mofield & Phelps, 2020). This extra 'tier' of learning at each station allows for further differentiation to adjust a specific activity 'up' or 'down' based on student readiness levels, just as a carousel moves up and down within its own rotation. Within an online meeting space, the different stations of learning can be managed through different breakout rooms (Webinar, 2020): Teacher led, Co-Teacher led, Collaborative Flexible Group Work, Independent Work.

Online Formative Assessments and Ongoing Feedback

While using technology to motivate and engage gifted and advanced learners, it is imperative to provide them with consistent, purposeful, and constructive feedback. It is near impossible to provide feedback, however, without meaningful formative assessments throughout a unit of study. Regardless of the setting (e.g., blended classroom, distance, hybrid, etc.), look for ways to engage students in formative assessments which continue to guide instruction and allow for the opportunity to communicate and/or demonstrate their levels of learning. From the formative assessments, feedback can be provided verbally or through written communication, but its purpose should help students recognize their areas of strength, as well as areas for growth. Table 1.4 provides sample ideas to use as formative assessments through readily available technology tools.

Table 1.3 Online Pre-assessment Strategies

Pre-Assessment Method	Description
Concept-Map	Concept-mapping is an easily integrated option for pre-assessing student readiness levels. Through distance learning, this can be accomplished through online concept-mapping applications (e.g., Concept Map Maker, MindMup, etc.) or through the student creation of concept maps through Google Docs or similar, or by simply having students create a concept map by paper and pencil and scanning or taking a picture to upload into the appropriate learning management system (e.g., Google Classroom, Canvas, Blackboard, etc.).
Google Forms	Use the 'quiz' feature of Google Forms to create a pre-assessment of content from already created assessments or create a pre-assessment based on desired learning objectives. All collected data is automatically input into a spreadsheet for easy reference.
Google Docs	By using a Google Doc or similar online document, students can respond to guiding questions about a particular unit of study. From the depth of a student's response, it is much easier to assess the level of mastery a student might already have about the content. Questions might include: ♦ What are five key vocabulary terms associated with this topic, what do they mean, and why are they integral to understanding this topic? ♦ When creating a unit test on this topic, what are three questions that should be included? Make sure to provide the answer key as part of your response. ♦ How does this unit of study connect with the universal themes and generalizations (e.g., power, change, chaos vs. order, exploration, etc.)?
Kahoot or Quizlet	Create a Kahoot or Quizlet by using multiple choice questions from an already developed pre-assessment or questions from an end of unit assessment. By using Kahoot as a pre-assessment, students are engaged in the process and data is gathered and tabulated for the teacher. Be mindful that Kahoot is a timed assessment measure focused on choice answers, so this is not an optimal option for analysis or assessment of content where multiple answers are acceptable. The 'time' factor could also lead to rushed vs. thoughtful responses.

Table 1.4 Sample Formative Assessment Technology Tools

Technology Tool	Formative Assessment
Google Forms	◆ Create questions to gauge students' levels of understanding. Questions can include open response, multiple choice, linear scale, checkboxes, etc. (See more on Google Forms in Chapter 3). All student responses are submitted directly back to the teacher to help further guide student learning. ◆ Create surveys to determine future areas of study or to assess students' current levels of understanding.
Google Docs/ Google Slides	◆ Create entry slips or exit slips to assess students' current levels of understanding and/or pre-assess for future lessons. Use 'comments' to provide appropriate feedback to support continued student learning.
Padlet	◆ Ask students to respond with insights, ideas, questions, etc. that relate to the current topic of study.
Penzu	◆ Provide opportunities for students to reflect on where they are in their learning. Potential reflection questions could include: • Which areas have been most difficult for me in my current learning and what have I done to persevere? • What unanswered questions do I still have regarding this topic? • What have I learned that conflicts with my previous level of understanding? • How does this learning connect with my personal life experiences? • If I could change one part of this learning module it would be _____ because _____.
Quizlet/ Kahoot/ etc.	◆ Create quick 'checking for understanding' quizzes to assess students' current levels of understanding.
Online Meeting Space Formatives	◆ Zoom in, Zoom out: Students move close to the camera for high levels of understanding and move far away from the camera to indicate lower levels of understanding with the topic. ◆ Thumbs Up/Thumbs Down: Students indicate levels of understanding by showing a thumbs up or thumbs down. ◆ Bitmoji/Emoji Scale: Students indicate level of understanding by a visual bitmoji rating scale, OR they physically 'make' an emoji face to indicate their personal levels of understanding. ◆ Meme/GIF Levels of Understanding: Students select a meme or GIF to indicate their personal levels of understanding.

Consistent online formative assessments also provide much needed check-in points for students. This continues to further develop and strengthen gifted and advanced students' psychosocial skills of time management, accountability, goal setting, and perseverance.

The Power of Reflection in Online Learning

In addition to providing ongoing feedback to your students through the use of technology, it is just as important to provide them with the opportunity to be reflective in their own learning. While there are many ways to accomplish this, there is no reason to make this more difficult than it needs to be. All students need to do is to share their reflections through Google docs, Penzu, or other similar applications and tools. Google Docs is especially useful because comments can be made directly to specific details within the reflection.

As with any learning, it is important to have clear expectations for what a strong reflection consists of. In addition to discussing these expectations with your students, consider posting a sample for students to see the difference between a strong reflection and a reflection that does not meet established expectations (see Table 1.5). It is often helpful to provide a list of guiding questions to help students in their online reflections. These might include:

Table 1.5 Student Reflection Examples

Weak Example	Strong Example
This activity was a lot of fun! I learned a lot of new things, and it wasn't boring. I think the part I liked most was when I could choose how I wanted to answer the final question. That part was cool!	*I found learning about sustainable energy to be very interesting because I did not realize how much it affects my own life. The part that surprised me the most was the amount of energy that wind can produce in West Texas! I also enjoyed being able to create a visual metaphor to demonstrate my new levels of understanding because it gave me an opportunity to use my artistic skills to share my learning. It also made me really have to think about the most important parts of what I learned and how I could show that visually. Even though that was harder than just writing a paragraph, I liked it so much more! I wish I could have learned more about how wind energy can be harnessed over large bodies of water, and I think I might even read a little bit more about that on my own. I was least interested in solar energy because I feel like I already know a lot about that.*

- What was the most interesting part of this project?
- What did you find the most difficult? How did you work through this aspect of the task?
- If you could change one part of this assignment, what would it be and why?
- What did you learn that was surprising or went against a personal assumption you had on this topic?
- What do you think was missing from this assignment? Why would it be important to include this component in the future?
- How did the use of technology enhance/distract your learning of the material?
- How did you use your personal strengths to accomplish this task?
- What real-world connections can you make to the learning in this task?

The Basics: In Review

Throughout this chapter, a focus has been given to recognizing the motivational and engagement needs of gifted and advanced learners in online and blended learning. In understanding these needs, along with the role of instructional technology, one is better able to evaluate readily available online resources to best meet the advanced needs for this population.

All too often, however, the 'free' and ready to use online resources are lacking, necessitating the need to understand how to move forward with adapting curriculum to be used through online or blended instruction or even designing your own online gifted curricula. By using the foundation of the What, How, Why: Then Justify approach to curricular design, pre-assessing for levels of readiness in learning, and utilizing ongoing formative assessments and reflection, gifted and advanced learners are provided with greater opportunities to engage in deeper levels of critical thinking through advanced online instruction. The following chapters will provide a greater context for integrating student collaborations, simulations, escape rooms, and other various instructional methods to the online instructional space, as well as providing guidance and support for parents and guardians as collaborative partners in online learning.

Chapter 2

Online Collaboration and Interaction

While blended and hybrid learning provide an "in-person" opportunity to build relationships and interact with each other while in a traditional setting, creating personal connections solely through distance learning is often a challenge. This not only applies to the connection between the teacher and the student, but also to the relationships between the students, themselves, as they engage and collaborate on various learning tasks. Regardless of whether you are setting up a traditional classroom, a completely online distance classroom, or a blended learning environment, a positive and inclusive learning environment should be established. As such, developing strong communication practices and clear expectations from the onset of online learning is paramount.

Creating a Collaborative Classroom Community

Technology can open many doors in education. When not appropriately implemented, however, it can potentially have a negative impact on students' interests, behaviors, value systems, and motivational attributes, as was often the case through the COVID-19 pandemic of 2020 when distance learning was mandated, not chosen. Within a traditional classroom environment, it is much easier to engage in conversations as students arrive to class, observe their body language as they are being introduced to new content, witness their successes, and support them through their frustrations in real time as they engage in completing their learning tasks. This is much more of a challenge through distance learning.

Another challenge of distance learning is helping gifted and advanced students feel connected to one another while they engage in the learning process. While some flourish in a distance learning environment, others struggle in not having the appropriate structures, supports, and supplies in place to help them succeed. One way to address this concern is through learning more about our students' backgrounds, interests, strengths, areas for growth, and value systems (Webinar, 2020). Through this, we are better prepared to design

DOI: 10.4324/9781003238317-2

online instruction to better meet their needs while also seeking opportunities for collaborative learning (Stargardter, 2020).

Value systems provide a context to gauge how students approach different learning tasks and why they choose to engage more readily with different types of learning activities. In essence, Wigfield and Eccles (2002) link motivation to how individuals value the tasks that they are asked to complete. This is further supported in knowing that academically gifted students report a lack of motivation when provided with learning activities that are uninteresting, too easy, or as lacking relevance to their areas of interest (Fredricks et al., 2010) More specifically, expectancy-value theory provides a greater understanding of the different types of value that students place on their learning (Wigfield & Eccles, 2002). Each of these is helpful in recognizing how to structure online learning tasks to better engage gifted and advanced learners:

- **Attainment value:** When students value learning through attainment value, they see the relevance and value of how the learning task is connected to their own sense of identity and "self." Whether a student identifies as a scholar, musician, athlete, or philosopher, connecting to students' personal identities is one way to elicit greater engagement in online learning.
- **Intrinsic value:** While intrinsic value is often closely associated with attainment value, it does not always connect directly to an individual's sense of self. Intrinsic value focuses on an individual's interests and is a common differentiation tool in terms of providing student choice in learning.
- **Utility value:** Through integrating utility value in online learning, students are more motivated and engaged to participate in learning tasks that are focused on how current learning will affect them in their future. This might be related to future course work (e.g., taking an AP course as an opportunity to earn college credit) or future vocational aspirations (e.g., integrating STEM because a student wishes to pursue a job in that field).
- **Cost:** While cost does not address a specific attribute of learning that will further motivate and sustain student engagement, it examines the other side of the "value" coin. What is the perceived sacrifice that a student must make to engage in the learning task? For example, what is the student going to have to "give up" in order to complete the assigned online learning task (e.g., video games with friends, time on social media, reading a favorite book, streaming a favorite series). When designing online learning for gifted and advanced learners, it is important to increase the value of learning such that it overrides the perceived cost of the other external factors that impact motivation.

Through a greater understanding of these different components of task valuation, these various value systems might be incorporated into online learning by allowing such things as student choice in research topics, selection of texts, choice boards (see Chapter 6), or placing students in online collaborative groups based on shared values to further engage and sustain involvement in online learning.

The question then becomes, "How do we ascertain which value systems our gifted and advanced students relate to the most?" The great news is that learning this information just involves some small tweaks to a common teacher tool: The Interest Inventory. Through careful considerations of question development, the "old school" interest inventory opens up doors to increasing gifted and advanced learners' motivation and subsequent engagement with online learning. The following section will provide additional information on not only how to assess task valuation through traditional interest inventories, but also how interest inventories lead to further collaborative opportunities through online learning.

Interest Inventories as a Trajectory for Online Collaboration

While many teachers continue to use the traditional interest inventories to learn more about their students, the use of technology opens up new and innovative venues for gleaning this information. In turn, alternative interest inventories also serve as a means to help students learn more about each other, as well. This not only continues to build a strong classroom community for online instruction, but it also helps to guide future collaborative learning experiences. In essence, the more the class is able to make connections with each other, the more they will feel comfortable working together through distance learning. Likewise, these various activities also provide greater insight to students' backgrounds, interests, and task valuation systems, better equipping the teacher to create engaging, challenging, and purposeful online learning opportunities.

Interest Inventories: Purposeful Selection

As you evaluate which online interest inventory is best for learning more about your students, it is equally important for your students to understand the purpose in the activity. Often, gifted and advanced learners view interest inventories as the meaningless hoops to jump through at the beginning of a school year that are placed into a file never to be seen again. These usually consist of surface level questions such as *What is your favorite subject?* Instead, questions should be created to allow for students to share more about what they hope to learn, why it is important to them, and how they see content connecting to their own lives. As with any learning task, continue to help students understand how this information will be used as a means to guide instruction, create connections, and make learning more relevant to their lives.

At the most basic level, interest inventories can be created through Google Forms. Whether you decide to use favorite questions from a past interest inventory or you decide to create new questions to learn more about your students and their task-valuation of learning, make sure the questions are purposeful and provide the type of information to help guide future instruction and create opportunities for deeper engagement in learning. The National Research Center on the Gifted and Talented (McCoach, n.d.) provides sample questions and suggestions for developing these types of questions to assess for the attainment, intrinsic, utility, and cost factors of task valuation. Questions might include:

- When I am learning, I see how this will help me to ___.
- I value learning about ___ because ___.
- I am most proud of my learning when given the opportunity to ___.
- I feel best/worst about my learning when ___.

Further questions can be found at:

♦ https://nrcgt.uconn.edu/underachievement_study/goal-valuation/gv_section0

Through Google Forms, student responses are collected and easily accessed by the teacher, but would not be visible to the class, as a whole. This provides a safety net for many students to feel more open to share more vulnerable aspects of themselves as learners, but it might not be the means to help students learn more about each other. Because of this, it is also recommended to provide students with opportunities to share more about themselves through community-building assignments. These opportunities provide more nontraditional options which some gifted and advanced learners might embrace more readily.

Table 2.1 provides suggestions for additional activities to learn more about your students and for your students to learn more about each other. The included tasks allow for greater depths of creativity and personalization, while also opening the door for both verbal and nonverbal expressions of individualization. With any of these tasks, it is important to communicate that the purpose of the activity is to help the class learn more about each other, while also helping the teacher discover how to better meet their learning needs throughout the year. In addition, for any of the options included in Table 2.1, students could also include an additional written overview for the activity and/or could share-out their assignment(s) as part of a class activity.

Whether you decide to use any of these suggested tasks or decide to utilize a different approach, consider providing *choice* as you continue to establish a culture of respect and acceptance from the onset of the school year. In addition, it is highly recommended that the teacher model how they would complete the chosen activity as a means to model what is expected while also continuing to introduce themselves to their class. As students engage in these tasks, consider using the following guiding questions:

♦ What am I interested in?
♦ What do I hope to accomplish in my future?
♦ What are my hobbies and special skills?
♦ How do I learn best?
♦ What is important to me in my life?
♦ What is important to me in my learning?
♦ What are some of my greatest accomplishments? (These could include non-tangible accomplishments like overcoming a fear of speaking in front of a group or taking a risk to try something new and unknown.)

With the information gained from these various approaches, it also opens the door to begin small group work with your students. Students can be placed into groups based on common interests to begin to build collaborative relationships. For instance, students might be placed in a group because they all indicated they are interested in animals or perhaps they like outdoor activities or sports. These are the first steps in finding commonalities to encourage student engagement and collaboration.

Table 2.1 Purposeful and Engaging Nontraditional Online Interest Inventories

Activity	Description
Virtual Lockers	Virtual Lockers allow students the opportunity to create "online" lockers which serve as visual representations of their own interests, accomplishments, hobbies, and backgrounds. While there are ample online examples of this, at its most basic level, students can use Google Slides to create a Bitmoji character and locker in the same manner that teachers create Bitmoji classrooms. In doing so, they are able to visually showcase items, posters, books, etc. in their virtual locker as a means to introduce themselves to their teacher and classmates.
Color Collage	This task includes students choosing one color and creating a collage of pictures that are predominately in that color. All pictures must represent who they are as a learner and an individual (see earlier suggested guiding questions). While it might sound a bit overwhelming, a Google image search allows students to select a color to guide their search. In essence, the student would type key search words into Google images and select the chosen color to guide the search results.
Double Acrostic	The double acrostic allows the student to respond to who they are as an individual through writing. In this case, they could use their name or a given word such as LEARN to tell more about themselves. With being a Double Acrostic, each letter in the chosen word must start AND end each sentence. For example, for the letter "L", a student might write: *Learning comes easily for me, but I am most engaged in my learning when I feel like the assignment is meaningful and purposefuL.* The student would continue to share more in subsequent sentences that begin AND end with the remaining letters in the chosen word. In this example, the following sentences would begin AND end with the letters E, A, R, and N. This adds a nice level of complexity to the task while also learning more about each student.
I Am From Poem	Inspired by the poem, *Where I'm From,* by George Ella Lyon, *I Am From* poems are a nice way to learn more about students' backgrounds, cultures, traditions, and sense of identity. Through the use of descriptive language and personal connections, students are able to learn more about each other. Providing a template and sentence stems is often helpful and continues to support multilingual learners. See Table 2.2 for student sample.
Video Introductions	For students who have access to video recording, consider having students create a short video introducing themselves.

(Continued)

Table 2.1 (Continued)

Activity	Description
	This might include question stems that students could use to guide their recordings, as well as suggested categories to include about themselves.
Me Mural	The Me Mural is very similar to the Color Collage, without the added constraint of "color." The student is able to search for images, words, and any other visual representations which respond to the guiding questions. As a result, a visual collage representing who they are as an individual is created.

Creating Online Collaborative Communities

When technology is utilized as an instructional tool within a traditional or blended classroom, it is much easier to provide personalized feedback and integrate in-person interactions as students are engaged in the learning process. Similarly, online learning as an extension of classroom learning or hybrid instruction also has a natural interaction between the teacher and students as they return to brick and mortar classrooms and discuss their progress with the various online learning tasks. Not only do these conversations allow for consistent feedback, they also encourage collaborative discussions and continue to motivate advanced and gifted learners to continue in their virtual quests of learning.

Distance learning, however, introduces a new set of challenges while creating and maintaining teacher/student relationships. This is further complicated by additional variables that impact student engagement and achievement while away from the traditional classroom setting (e.g., parental support, access to technology, an unstructured learning environment) leading to possible underachievement in gifted and advanced students. How then, can these relationships be best established and maintained through online interactions?

The Importance of Environment

At the onset of distance learning, the top priority should be to establish a safe and collaborative online learning environment. The NAGC (2019) Programming Standards address the importance of environment for gifted and advanced learners through:

♦ Fostering a love for learning
♦ Encouraging personal and social responsibility
♦ Ensuring multicultural competence
♦ Strengthening interpersonal and technical communications skills for leadership

While distance learning is not a traditional classroom setting, it *is* a classroom setting with its own learning environment, and how the learning environment is established will impact how the students remain engaged, take risks in their learning, and continue to work up to their potential.

Table 2.2 I Am From Poem: 6th-Grade Student Work Sample

> I am from love and trust
> and parents who believe in me.
> I am from the warmth
> down in the south.
> The smell of sand and dirt
> whipping around you as you drive on unknown roads.
> Cowboys? Tumbleweeds?
> Yes, but not exactly that.
> I am from the Lord's family,
> where he answers our prayers
> and renews our faith.
> I am from dolls
> and bears,
> from blankets and bibs.
> I am from spending all day in a baby pool
> and playing in a tree house,
> from singing songs on the swings.
> I am from taking an extra cookie
> with a smirk on my face
> and never being able to have
> enough of Grandma's mac n' cheese.
> I am from silly songs and sayings,
> patience and annoyance.
> From "Here we sit like birds in the wilderness" to
> "If you mess with the bull be prepared for the horns."
> Under my bed would be junk to others,
> but to me it is memories.
> Albums filled with pictures
> that remind me of older times.
> I am from loyalty and togetherness,
> without it,
> I wouldn't be who I am today.

For some distance learning scenarios, students have already had some interactions within the traditional classroom setting and simply need the opportunity to reestablish themselves within the new distance learning model of instruction. This can be done by building upon the connections that have already been established through student participation in online activities that help them feel comfortable in using various online tools and applications (e.g., creating avatars, engaging in online meeting forums, using various online tools to complete assignments based on interest or personalized content). In other scenarios, distance learning is established from the onset of the school year, and creating activities to build a sense of community becomes even more important. Table 2.3 provides suggestions for how to build and sustain an environment as a Collaborative Online Community.

Table 2.3 Tasks for Establishing Collaborative Online Communities

Community-Building Task	Description of Task
Community Circle	Through an online meeting space (e.g., Zoom, TEAMS) a Community Circle allows an opportunity to greet one another, make announcements, and set the tone for learning that day. While most commonly used in elementary classrooms, a more condensed version of this "community dialogue" is also beneficial at the intermediate levels. During Community Circle, each student might have the opportunity to share a quick thought about something that is on their mind, a common question might be asked to the class, or students might respond to a current event. Regardless of the conversation starter, all students are given an opportunity to share, and students are also allowed to pass if they do not care to share. As a safe learning environment continues to develop, more and more students will actively participate in Community Circle sharing time.
Would You Rather	This popular game started out as a board game, but now "Would You Rather" questions are easily found online. The whole purpose of this activity is to present students with two extreme questions, to which students choose one of the options and explain why. For example, *Would you rather be a little late or way too early?* or *Would you rather have fingernails that were 12 inches long or hair that dragged the ground?* Not only do these types of questions serve as nice icebreakers, they also encourage creative dialogue. Gifted and advanced learners often enjoy submitting their own "Would You Rather" questions for use within a classroom.
Puzzle Party	From Google Arts & Culture: https://artsandculture.google.com/experiment/puzzle-party/EwGBPZlIzv 0KRw
	Puzzle Party provides an opportunity to collaboratively work an online puzzle together through a shared link. There are many puzzle options and three different difficulty levels. While puzzle working is often viewed as a quiet, independent activity, it provides a non-threatening space to continue to build a sense of community and collaboration with gifted and advanced learners. Your students might just need a space to build

(Continued)

Table 2.3 (Continued)

Community-Building Task	Description of Task
	community by collaboratively working toward a common goal by completing a puzzle together, or there are additional ways to add a little extra pizzazz to the Puzzle Party collaborative experience. Here are just a few suggestions: ♦ Select the "Hide Preview" option at the bottom of the screen and have students predict what the final image will be. This is especially entertaining with the more difficult puzzle options. ♦ Consider using puzzle building to review or reinforce skills or content through metaphors or similes. In this variation, students would create a metaphor or simile connecting the image on the puzzle to a current unit of study. You will be amazed at the connections they make! ♦ Have students think more abstractly about the image of the puzzle by asking them to make connections to universal themes and generalizations (i.e., power, change, order vs. chaos, exploration, etc.).
Padlet Perplexity	One way to encourage creativity while also learning more about each other as a community of learners is to play a version of 2 Truths and a Lie, called Padlet Perplexity. This version has the same premise of the traditional game where each student creates two or more facts that are true and one fact that is not. The rest of the class then guesses which of the "facts" is the untruth. By using Padlet as the venue, it adds something a little different into the mix and also familiarizes students with this platform for use in future learning tasks.

Setting the Stage for Respectful and Accountable Talk

Thus far, this chapter has discussed the importance of learning more about students as a means to build community, as well as the impact of the environment on strengthening community and setting the stage for successful student collaboration. All of this would fall to the wayside, however, if respectful and accountable talk was not at the foundation of the learning environment, itself.

With so much focus on learning standards, academic content, integration of technology, and the remaining plethora of teaching responsibilities, taking the time to explicitly teach accountable talk can easily be overlooked. While we want to believe that all of our students come to school prepared with strong interpersonal skills, this often is not the case. Taking the time to integrate mini lessons focused on accountable talk through online learning is imperative to successful online instruction. This includes teaching gifted and advanced students *how* to communicate with their peers on collaborative projects, within breakout rooms, through online comments/posts, or while engaging in discussions through online meeting spaces or chat rooms. Providing sentence stems for accountable talk continues to guide these conversations while also supporting multilingual learners. Examples of accountable talk sentence stems might include:

- I agree with ____ because _____.
- I disagree with that because _____.
- I want to add to what (name) said about _____.
- Based on my evidence, I think _____.
- A question I have is _____.
- Clarify what you mean by _____.
- This reminds me of _____.

As the saying goes, "If you have met one gifted student, you have met one gifted student." There are gifted and advanced learners who are extremely introverted and need consistent encouragement to share their insights and thoughts on a topic of study. There are others, who have a difficult time listening to others because they think they already have all of the answers and their way is the *only* way, and of course there are all those students that fall between these two ends of the spectrum. Regardless of the type of learner, it is helpful to model and provide guidance on how to best navigate collaborative conversations. Table 2.4 provides suggestions on how to encourage collaborative conversations. In most online learning environments, breakout rooms provide an easily managed space for these tasks. While these are just a small sampling of ideas to encourage collaborative conversations, the objective is for students to practice collaboration with their peers.

Collaborative Projects

While continuing to create a sense of community and further develop interpersonal skills in online learning, it is also important to provide opportunities for students to work collaboratively on assignments, projects, and other various learning tasks. Regardless of the activity, remain mindful that students are working through the What, How, Why: Then Justify approach (see Chapter 1) to ensure a greater depth of learning. Also, continue to evaluate which collaborative learning tasks from a traditional classroom setting might be easily adapted to online learning. For example, preparing for and engaging with a debate encourages strong collaborative involvement, as debate "teams" conduct research, develop their arguments, and prepare for counter-arguments. Through online learning, gifted and advanced learners could continue debate preparation in separate break-out rooms, while organizing their thoughts on a shared platform (e.g., Google Doc, Jamboard, Outlook), and the debate, itself, could be held through an online meeting space, such as Zoom or TEAMS. Other collaborative opportunities for online learning include:

Table 2.4 Strategies for Encouraging Collaborative Conversations

Strategy	Description
Think Then Talk (TTT)	TTT is much like a Think, Pair, Share approach, in the way that it first requires each learner to think independently before engaging in collaborative talk. Once each student thinks AND writes their own thoughts on a topic, each student then takes turns sharing their thoughts with the group. Each member of the collaborative group is only given a certain amount of time to share without interruption before it is the next student's turn. As each student is done sharing, the other group members are encouraged to affirm what the current student shared before allowing the next student their turn in sharing. This strategy is useful in encouraging all students' voices to be equally heard, while also encouraging active listening.
Keeping Perspective Through Perspectives	When using this strategy, each student is assigned a certain perspective that they must use when engaging in collaborative conversations. This might be through de Bono's Six Thinking Hats (see Chapter 1) or through different stakeholders' (e.g., parent, law officer, student, scientist) perspectives. This approach continues to encourage the importance of all voices being discussed and analyzed by providing different types of insights and areas of focus.
The Missing Link	Through this strategy, each student is provided with a different integral piece of information that is needed to successfully solve a problem/mystery or answer a guiding question. Students are required to verbally share their information. Most often used in solving math problems or mysteries, this approach to collaborative conversations requires that students use active listening and effective communication to work together toward a common goal.
Role-Play	Role-playing provides students with various scenarios that they must act out in the appropriate manner. These situations might include how to talk through conflict, how to ask for help when you are unsure of next steps, or how to share feelings about a particular situation.

(Continued)

Table 2.4 (Continued)

Strategy	Description
ABC Collaboration	Adapted from Richard Cash's (2016) Affective, Behavioral, and Cognitive Self-Regulation Learning Model, students are able to engage in collaborative conversations where they communicate their affect (feelings), their behaviors, and their cognition (thinking/metacognition) about a particular topic.

- Literature Circles based on readiness levels through breakout rooms
- Creating a collaborative piece of writing (e.g., expository text, mathematics solution manual, scientific lab report after an online dissection simulation)
- Socratic Seminars based on readiness levels through breakout rooms
- Presentation development (e.g., Google Slides, Prezi, Infographic)
- Culminating projects (e.g., online museum exhibit, Google Sites development on a specific topic, podcast, virtual showcase [see Chapter 6], documentary)

Chapter 6 includes additional options that can easily be integrated into online collaborative work, as well, but regardless of the assigned collaborative task, it is important to have clear expectations while also providing consistent and meaningful feedback to each collaborative group. Likewise, in the next three chapters, there are additional opportunities for collaborative work through online escape rooms and simulations. While these also work well as autonomous learning modules, collaborative learning is always an option.

Chapter 3

Using Google Forms as Accountable and Engaging Learning Modules

Without question, Google Forms is a valuable tool when looking to collect responses and evaluate data from student work. It also offers the ability to create self-graded quizzes, graph data, and provide students with an opportunity to work independently through online learning. Unfortunately, however, the needs of gifted and advanced learners are often not considered when designing and implementing Google Forms, leading to a lack of motivation, disengagement, and underachievement. This chapter focuses on how to design and implement online learning through Google Forms with gifted pedagogy as the foundation.

Because Google Forms is so versatile, it is easy to fall into the trap of taking the path of least resistance. This includes using Google Forms as the equivalent of a scantron sheet or limiting the degree of difficulty to ensure that students are easily "successful" in obtaining the correct answer while working independently on any online learning task. Not only does this perpetuate the problem of gifted and advanced learners not having access to challenging learning experiences, it also continues to deprive them of opportunities to engage with the productive struggle needed to cultivate perseverance and other important psychosocial skills (e.g., time management, goal setting, self-advocacy). When reflecting on what is best practice for gifted and advanced learners, the NAGC (2019) Programming Standards continue to reinforce that gifted and advanced students need to:

♦ Be provided with high-level programming through digital learning options
♦ Have opportunities for accelerated learning
♦ Learn through multiple approaches, instructional strategies, and talent development explorations
♦ Engage through evidence-based curricular resources

DOI: 10.4324/9781003238317-3

The Basics

Through careful consideration of content and instructional strategies, Google Forms is versatile enough to encompass many of these standards. Before sharing how to design purposeful and meaningful learning experiences through Google Forms, it is important to address a few of the Google Forms' settings and design applications. Table 3.1 shares several of the key navigational features found at the top of any Google Forms' application.

As referenced above, once the basic navigational components are understood, then it is time to begin exploring the various options for how to develop Google Forms as a meaningful instructional tool. This is the stage of design where the needs of gifted and advanced learners are often overlooked. To help guide this phase of curriculum development, Table 3.2 includes the various Google Forms' options and shares the aligning gifted considerations for use. While these suggestions are not exhaustive, they do provide a quick reference of how to utilize this tool while designing lessons for gifted and advanced learners.

Transforming Existing Lessons

Much of the existing curricula utilized in schools do not always address the needs of gifted and advanced learners (Braunshausen, 2017), leading to underachievement and potential behavior manifestations. In fact, gifted students, themselves, have voiced that they are seeking innovative lessons which actively engage them in the learning process (Phelps, in press), and Google Forms provides the opportunity to transform existing lessons into innovative online learning modules. Whether you are looking to create engaging escape rooms or provide a context for simulations, Google Forms offers flexibility in learning tasks while also providing a much-needed structure for assessing student progress and growth.

At its most basic level, any type of question/response can be structured through Google Forms. As previously mentioned, the same level of attention needs to go into planning an appropriately challenging learning experience for gifted and advanced learners as what is required through traditional paper and pencil assignments. Students' readiness levels should be considered, appropriately challenging content should be incorporated, and students should be given ample opportunity to engage in critical thinking and problem-solving through open-ended questions. As such, continue to refer to Table 3.2 when transforming existing lessons into Google Forms for gifted and advanced learners. Also continue to be mindful of the "What, How, Why: Then Justify" approach (see Chapter 1). This is easily incorporated by selecting the appropriate question format and continues to incorporate ongoing reflection as part of the learning process.

Table 3.1 Key Navigational Features of Google Forms

Google Form Feature	Explanation of Use
Theme Options	◆ Select Header Image ◆ Select Theme Color ◆ Select Background Color ◆ Select Font Style
Preview	◆ Allows any creator/editor of the Google Form to see and work through the "student" view. (This becomes very important as a means to "work through" or "practice" any escape room or simulation learning experience prior to assigning to students.)
Settings	◆ Provides selection for the type of Google Form: General, Presentation, or Quiz. (Presentation and Quiz mode offer further selections.) ◆ Select if email addresses should be collected (This is important in identifying who has submitted what response.) ◆ Select if Response Receipts will be provided ◆ Limit Responses ◆ Allow/Disallow additional edits after submissions
Send	◆ Select if Form will be shared/accessed through email, shared link, or hyperlink ◆ Select if email addresses should be collected (This is important in identifying who has submitted what response.) ◆ Add collaborators (e.g., co-teachers, special education teachers, ELL teachers) This is valuable in co-planning and co-teaching.
More Options	◆ Undo option ◆ Make a copy ◆ Move to trash ◆ Print ◆ Add collaborators (e.g., co-teachers, special education teachers, ELL teachers). This is valuable in co-planning and co-teaching. ◆ Other various options
"Questions"	By selecting "Questions" at the top of the Google Form, one is able to begin to develop the questions to be included as part of this option.
"Responses"	By selecting "Responses" at the top of the Google Form, one is able to accept responses, see responses, and manage responses through download or print options.

Table 3.2 Gifted Considerations for Use with Google Forms Tasks

Icon	Task	Gifted Considerations for Use
⊕	Add Question	♦ Focus on higher level questioning (e.g., higher levels of Bloom's Taxonomy, Depth of Knowledge Levels 3 and 4) ♦ Steer away from multiple-choice options in regard to content. Instead, provide open-ended questions to ensure students have the opportunity to synthesize advanced content and justify their reasoning. ♦ Create questions that allow students to connect advanced content to universal themes and generalizations (see Chapter 1). ♦ Be mindful to incorporate depth (e.g., trends, unanswered questions, ethical concerns, patterns) and complexity (e.g., change over time, multiple points of view, connections to other disciplines) into your questions (Kaplan, 2009).
⤇	Import Question	♦ Import existing questions from successful gifted curriculum units you have used in the past. ♦ Import questions from standard curriculum options and further modify them to better meet the needs of gifted and advanced learners. Remain mindful of supports for multilingual learners.
Tт	Add Title and Description	♦ This is your "hook" to grab your students' attention. Be creative and pique your students' curiosity! ♦ Be concise in your descriptions. The goal is to engage your students so that they will be motivated to continue!
▣	Add Image	♦ Adding images helps to personalize the often-bland appearance of Google Forms. Have fun with this and think about adding some images that will bring a smile to your students' faces! ♦ Consider creating an ongoing theme through image selection (e.g., space travel, historical time period, dinosaurs)
▶	Add Video	♦ Consider adding videos to introduce and/or reinforce the lesson's focus (e.g., read-alouds, scientific experiments, demonstrations, documentary segments). ♦ Videos can be pulled from online sources such as YouTube, or you can include videos that you or your students have created.
▤	Add Section	♦ Adding sections to your Google Forms allows students to focus on one component of the learning module at a time, ensuring that students are taking the time to process the information rather than just rushing through the work.

(Continued)

Table 3.2 (Continued)

Icon	Task	Gifted Considerations for Use
		♦ Consider incorporating a culminating question or reflection at the end of each section to help students synthesize the provided content. Not only will this help them grow in their own conceptual understanding, it will also provide you with powerful formative assessment data to guide future instruction. ♦ Special note: Using this task transforms Google Forms into an online escape room or simulation (discussed later in this chapter).

Escape Rooms

Escape rooms have become all the rage over the past decade, including "in-person" experiences both inside and outside of the classroom. If you are unfamiliar with the escape room approach to learning, this instructional strategy presents students with "clues" to solve as they interact and engage with academic content. An escape room lesson, itself, is divided into different components, and before students are able to "unlock" the next component of learning, they must first use the available resources to solve a problem, answer a question, or decipher a code before moving on to the next steps of the learning experience.

Companies have taken advantage of this innovative instructional approach to engage people in collaborative problem-solving by selling online programming to be used with a series of locks, boxes, and other various tools. While many of these items can be found at home and/or purchased at discount stores, this approach to escape rooms is often difficult to implement and assess through online learning. While there are some "free" online escape rooms available for download, many of them do not provide the level of rigor and complexity needed to meet the needs of gifted and advanced learners, and those that are appropriately leveled often require an annual subscription. There are also some readily accessible applications, such as flippity.net, that provide students with the opportunity to "unlock" various locks based on answering questions correctly. Unfortunately, it is difficult to see the progression of student work through these various applications (i.e., formative assessments) to further guide instruction. This is where Google Forms comes in handy!

Whether you have escape room lessons that you have successfully used with gifted and advanced learners in the past or you have some novel ideas to create a new, original escape room learning experience, consider using Google Forms to engage your students as part of your online instruction. As you begin, the SOLVE Process (see Table 3.3) provides a structure to help guide escape room development for gifted and advanced learners.

Resource 3 provides a template to provide guidance during the planning stages of online escape room design. Once you have a well-developed instructional plan, it is now time to bring your escape room to life through Google Forms.

Table 3.3 The SOLVE Process for Successful Escape Room Design

Subject-area of focus	◆ What specific content will be the focus of this escape room? ◆ Does the topic provide an opportunity to have standards-based, measurable outcomes based on advanced content? ◆ In knowing the subject-area of focus, what type of scenario would be best to present the desired content? ◆ Are there cross-curricular/interdisciplinary connections that can be integrated?
Objectives of learning	◆ Specify the advanced learning objectives for the lesson (e.g., Students will be able to…; SWBAT). ◆ Identify key vocabulary, skills, events, etc. that can be assessed through this learning experience. How will students be able to actively engage with this content? ◆ Which specific advanced standards will be addressed?
Learning materials needed	◆ What types of materials do you already have and/or need to create for this lesson? Examples of materials might include: reading passages, math problems, images, video links, definitions, primary sources, etc.
Variety of clues to "unlock"	◆ Include a variety of methods to "unlock" next steps in learning (e.g., answer a question with an exact word, decipher a clue, embed a link or QR code to provide additional information in problem-solving, answer a content-specific riddle, fill in the blank, simplify a fraction, write a question backwards and have the student answer it backwards, complete a pattern, bold certain letters to be unscrambled). See next section for more information.
Evaluation of learning	◆ Provide an opportunity for self-reflection as a culminating component of the escape room experience. Consider asking: • What was the most challenging part of this escape room experience? • What did you learn that confirmed what you already thought or challenged any assumptions you might have had? • What unanswered questions do you still have as a result of this escape room experience? • How did you manage any frustrations of not immediately knowing the answers?

Resource 3 **SOLVE: Escape Room Planning Sheet**

Subject/Content Area:

Standards to be addressed:

Story or scenario for Escape Room experience (optional):

Objectives of learning (SWBAT):

Learning materials needed to achieve desired learning objectives (worksheets, links, images, graphs, texts, etc.):

Variety of clues to "unlock" Learning Modules:

Evaluation of learning:

Unlocking Escape Room Design

At its most basic level, an escape room through Google Forms is anchored in the types of questions and responses, utilized as the locks and keys to proceed through the learning challenge. By planning through the SOLVE Process as a means to organize integral components of the escape room experience, it is now time to consider how the specific questions will be developed. Keep in mind that escape rooms can be designed as autonomous learning modules or as collaborative learning experiences.

Whether questions are selected from an already established activity or website (e.g., breakoutedu.com) or are new and original, you will need to integrate "response validation" questions through Google Forms. This option requires students to enter an "exact" response before the next level of the online learning is made accessible. Within a traditional classroom's escape room experience, this would be represented by students "unlocking" a box to retrieve the next clue. The following section provides an overview of how these different question options in Google Forms can serve as your "locks" and "keys" in designing an online escape room.

Response Validation Guidance

While all question formats are able to be integrated as part of escape room design, the types of questions discussed below will serve as the "locks" for student progression throughout the online escape room experience. The subsequent student responses then serve as the keys to unlock the next portion of the learning experience.

Checkboxes

This type of question format presents students with a list of choices and provides three options to "unlock" the next level of play through response validation. These consist of: *Select at least*, *Select at most*, or *Select exactly*. While not being as specific as a standard multiple-choice question, the following suggestions provide a context for using this type of question with gifted and advanced learners:

♦ *After reading the selected text, what are the top three findings as stated from the research?* ("Select exactly" variation when used with advanced content through a complex text.)
♦ *When you think about your future vocational goals, which of the following are skills and/or subjects that are necessary components of that occupation? Select at least 3.* ("Select at least" variation when used to assess task valuation through attainment value. See Chapter 2.)

Paragraph

This type of response is selected when a question is more open-ended in nature, and the response requires a multiple line, greater length of detail. There are two variations of how this type of question can be utilized when used with "Response validation" to unlock the next phase of the escape room experience: *Length* and *Regular expression*.

By selecting a length requirement, the teacher designates a minimum or maximum character count to be required as part of the written response. For example, if greater levels of complexity are added to a response by placing additional constraints (e.g., including different types of figurative language, a particular number of words from another language, a particular number of five syllable words), then a minimum character count would be beneficial to ensure that all of the required components are included in the response. When considering the maximum length requirement, it is often just as challenging, if not more so, to limit a gifted or advanced learner's response to a maximum number of characters. By using the maximum length requirement, the difficulty of the response is increased by directing gifted and advanced learners to be concise in their writing, while still providing an in-depth written response. The following are examples of paragraph response validation questions to be used with gifted and advanced learners as part of an online escape room:

- *After reading the two shared poems, what similar themes do they share? Your response should be in paragraph form and include at least three forms of figurative language, at least two words that are five syllables long, and exactly one word from a different language.* (Length: "Minimum character count" variation)
- *What generalization can you make about the Civil War from reading the provided primary source documents? In paragraph form, share your generalization and justify your answer in less than 400 characters.* (Length: "Maximum character count" variation)

Response validation for paragraph response questions is also available through the "Regular expression" option. When using this format, the response options include: *Contains, Doesn't contain, Matches*, and *Doesn't match*. Each of these options indicates what a student response must have, or in some cases must *not* have to unlock the next level in the escape room experience.

Short Answer

This type of question allows for a single line of student response. In the context of an online escape room, this format serves as a lock and key when asking students to respond with a specific word, mathematical value, or phrase. This type of question is also useful when creating a "code" through a series of answers from preceding questions. For example, a short answer response could create a code by having students enter their responses, in order, from five previous multiple choice, True/False, matching, fill in the blank, numbered diagrams, or number value questions (e.g., TFFTT, ACBDA, 35791). The following are examples of response validation questions that could be used with gifted and advanced learners using the short answer response as code:

- *5 DIGIT NUMBER LOCK: Enter the binary equivalent for decimal number 24* (Equal to 11000).
- *LETTER LOCK: Enter the letters, in order, from the above matching exercise.*

Online Escape Rooms in a Blended Learning Environment

Through a distance model of online learning, the escape room is entirely conducted through the Google Forms' platform. When used in a blended model of online instruction, additional opportunities to enhance the escape room experience become more readily available. This is done by integrating and aligning additional learning components within the traditional classroom with the use of Google Forms as the "locks" and "keys" of the escape room experience. Various ideas of escape room integration in this manner include:

- Have students search for clues around the room to answer a Google Forms question to "unlock" the next task.
- Use a combination of real locks and keys with containers in the classroom with the virtual locks and keys as part of Google Forms.
- Integrate some random physical acts that a team of students must complete between questions (e.g., play a game of leapfrog around the room, complete ten jumping jacks, spell the word "fun" with their bodies, stack 15 cups).

Not only does this add an additional spark to the learning environment, it provides an opportunity for students to incorporate active movement into the learning process.

A Little Extra Pizzazz

Regardless of if escape rooms are implemented through a distance or blended model of instruction, continue to reflect on how to integrate elements that will engage gifted and advanced learners while also adding a little bit of extra pizzazz along the way. Many of these ideas stem from knowing your students' interests and integrating a little more creativity into the escape room experience.

As previously mentioned, integrating movement is a simple way to add physical activity into the learning process. Even if the escape room is being conducted entirely online, either independently or collaboratively through a virtual meeting space, consider adding a physical requirement as part of experience (e.g., touch your toes and crabwalk across the room). While this physical movement does not add to the academic complexity of the learning experience, physical activity does help with the thinking process (Madison, 2020; Mullender-Wignsma et al., 2015).

Gifted and advanced learners also find more value in learning when they see a connection to their own lives (Phelps, in press). As such, find ways to integrate students' interests into the escape room experience. For example, if students have interests in particular games, subject areas, clubs, movies, sports, etc., consider integrating those topics into a storyline for the escape room. This can also be enhanced by integrating pictures and using student names in a positive, encouraging manner. In summary, as you design an escape room experience, think about what your students would really enjoy. You will be amazed at how quick it is to create these learning experiences and subsequently, how engaged your gifted and advanced students will be!

Simulations

Online simulations through Google Forms can also provide gifted and advanced learners with an opportunity to engage in challenging learning experiences based on deeper levels of critical thinking. Similar to how an escape room is developed through creating response validation questions, a simulation can be created by incorporating different phases, or levels, that students must complete before proceeding to the next phase of the simulation.

While escape rooms benefit from having an integrated storyline, a storyline is an essential component to an online simulation. The storyline develops the context of learning throughout the entire experience while also providing an essential sense of identity for the learner, or participant, in the simulation experience. More explanation of using Google Forms as a simulation learning experience is provided in Chapter 4, and a continued focus of designing long-term online simulations for gifted and advanced learners through Google Sites is discussed in Chapter 5.

Providing Personalized Feedback

Whether Google Forms is used as a summative assessment, an escape room, or a simulation, it is important to provide meaningful and purposeful feedback to student work. Unlike Google Docs, there is not a "comment" feature on Google Forms, so it is necessary to be a little more creative with methods to provide constructive feedback. One way is by providing a rubric for students to see what is expected *prior* to engaging in this form of online learning and then using that rubric to communicate and provide additional feedback after the completion of the Google Forms assignment. This can be accomplished by sharing the rubric online during distance learning or sharing a hardcopy through the blended classroom.

Another approach includes using Resource 4 to respond to designated sections of Google Forms' learning modules. In this manner, each section of the learning activity is divided into sections focused on particular skills, and meaningful and constructive feedback can be better focused on specific skills or learning objectives. An electronic version of this form can be found at www.routledge.com/9781646322213 and is helpful for use with any Google Forms' submissions, including escape rooms and online simulations, which are discussed in more detail in Chapter 4.

Resource 4 Learning Module Feedback Document

Student Name:

Assignment:

Section ___ Overview/Questions: Provide a quick restatement of key components or questions from this learning module/section:
- ♦
- ♦
- ♦
- ♦

Learning Module ___ Feedback
- ♦
- ♦
- ♦
- ♦

Section ___ Overview/Questions: Provide a quick restatement of key components or questions from this learning module/section:
- ♦
- ♦
- ♦
- ♦

Learning Module ___ Feedback
- ♦
- ♦
- ♦
- ♦

Source: Created by Vicki Phelps.

Chapter 4

Brackets of Learning:
A Google Forms Simulation

While Chapter 3 discussed different considerations and applications for implementing Google Forms with gifted and advanced learners, this chapter provides step-by-step instructions for how to create and implement an entire simulation unit focused on teaching critical thinking skills and evaluative thinking. As such, this unit is useful in teaching a variety of advanced processing strategies at the beginning of the year as a means to introduce students to a variety of thinking models.

Taking the form of a "March Madness" tournament, the skills and critical thinking models are introduced through the context of the Guiding Question: *Who is the Greatest Hero?* While the people/characters of this bracket were adapted from Mensa's Hero Bracket Challenge (Brooks, 2010), the context of this simulation was created to introduce students to research-based processing models developed to engage and challenge gifted and advanced learners through an engaging simulation focused on critical thinking.

Throughout the Hero's Bracket Tournament, students are engaged through a training simulation geared to prepare them to become ACES Astronauts (Advanced Criteria Evaluation Specialists). In taking this instructional approach, gifted and advanced students are better engaged to interact with the content and sustain their focus for longer periods of time (Wigfield et al., 2004). This also opens the door for teachers to integrate humor and opportunities for creativity into the instructional design as a means to further engage students in learning.

As a quick overview, the unit is divided into six different learning modules, which allow each student to master one area before progressing to the next. This also provides the teacher with an opportunity to provide timely and meaningful feedback throughout the learning process, as well as make any needed modifications to learning, based-off of these formative assessment measures. The learning modules are structured in the following order:

1. Creating and Applying Criteria for Evaluative Decision-Making
2. Concept Mapping as a Problem-Solving Tool (Focus: Superheroes)
3. Elements of Reasoning (Focus: Theatrical Heroes)
4. Analytical Thinking (Focus: Literary Heroes)
5. Double Fishbone (Focus: Historical Heroes)
6. The Winner Is…

DOI: 10.4324/9781003238317-4

Processing Tools for Problem-Solving: An Overview

Each of the learning modules within this simulation focuses on providing gifted and advanced learners with the opportunity to engage with a variety of valuable processing tools as applied to problem-solving. Each learning module, whether introduced each day within a blended classroom or over a longer span of time through hybrid or distance learning environments, will guide gifted and advanced students through how to apply a new processing and thinking tool to better support strong, evaluative decision-making. The following sections provide a quick overview of the incorporated processing models.

The Role of Criteria on Evaluative Decision-Making

As a means to help gifted and advanced learners engage in effective and well-informed decision-making, Learning Module 1 focuses on introducing students to the importance of criteria in the evaluative thinking process. After first being presented with the guiding question, *Who is the Greatest Hero?*, students are introduced to criteria, including how to write and apply criteria to decision-making. Students begin to recognize that applying criteria to the evaluative thinking process helps to alleviate and address potential assumptions and biases. The student-created criteria from Learning Module 1 will be utilized throughout the remainder of the learning modules, continuing to provide a common thread of consistency throughout the simulation.

Concept Mapping as a Problem-Solving Tool

Concept mapping, often referred to as bubble mapping, is commonly used as a pre-writing or brainstorming activity where students group related terms through a series of connected lines and circles as a means to organize thoughts. It is also a helpful tool to encourage the dimensions of creative thinking: fluency, flexibility, originality, and elaboration (Guilford, 1986). Figure 4.1 provides an example of the beginning stages of a concept map focused on the topic of natural disasters.

Because of its versatility, concept mapping can also be used as a successful problem-solving tool by focusing the content on key facts, attributes, and supporting factors for the decision-making process. A concept map focused on problem-solving would designate the topic, problem, or issue, as the center circle, and the various solutions for the problem would stem out from that original circle. For example, if the center circle was focused on the problem of keeping people safe during hurricanes, the connecting circles would include the various ways to accomplish this task (e.g., sandbags, levees, evacuation plans, warning sirens, engineering buildings to sustain hurricanes). Each of these areas would be further developed with more connecting lines and circles containing further research and support. The area(s) with the most factual support, in conjunction with the guiding criteria (e.g.,

Figure 4.1 *Natural Disaster Concept Map Example.*

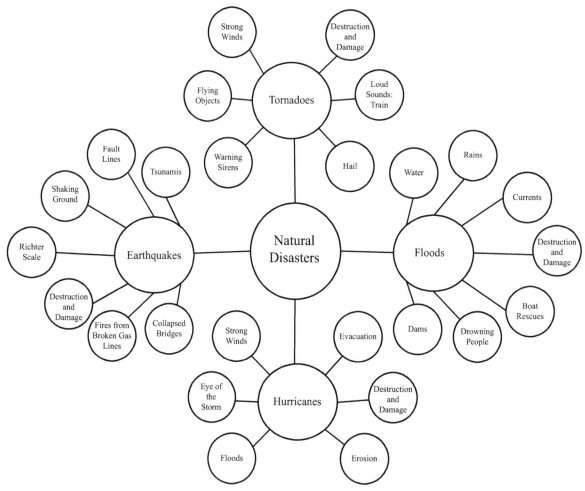

impact the most people, most economical, quickest to enact), would be helpful in evaluating the best solution to the problem. The chosen solution could then be further developed into a proposal for change.

Within this simulation, Learning Module 2 is focused on using a concept map as a means to evaluate and select the "best" superhero. By focusing on the different strengths, weaknesses, and backgrounds of the different superheroes, in conjunction with the criteria that was developed in Learning Module 1, students evaluate and decide which superhero should move forward to the next round of the bracket competition.

Evaluation through Elements of Reasoning

As students begin to evaluate which theatrical heroes best support the guiding criteria, Paul and Elder's (2019) elements of reasoning will be introduced as a processing model to further evaluate and determine which theatrical hero would be considered the strongest role model in teaching heroic traits to today's youth. This critical thinking model considers multiple parts, or elements of thinking, to further analyze and evaluate a particular content-focus through identifying questions, purpose, points of view, assumptions, concepts, information, inferences, and implications associated with that area of focus.

For Learning Module 3, students will focus on a portion of these elements by examining how varying perspectives, points of view, assumptions, and implications impact each of the identified theatrical heroes. More specifically, for the purpose of this learning module, various stakeholders (i.e., juvenile court judge, archaeologist, college professor, psychologist/mental health worker) will be identified to incorporate different perspectives of analysis. As a means to better understand the accompanying points of view, assumptions, and implications of the various stakeholders, an understanding of each of the stakeholder's education and job description will be explored to better support the necessary evaluative thinking that is required through this processing model.

Analysis with Applied Thinking Tools

Gifted and advanced learners also benefit from having opportunities to think critically and deeply about literature. Throughout Learning Module 4, gifted and advanced learners will use the Literary Analysis Wheel (Mofield & Stambaugh, 2016) to examine how "flexible" the various literary heroes are in response to the guiding criteria. More specifically, Learning Module 4 will guide gifted and advanced learners to examine the key interactions of setting, language, and symbols from chosen pieces of literature.

Students will then use their literary analysis in conjunction with the established criteria to determine which literary hero will proceed to the next round of the hero bracket challenge. While any reading selections can be integrated into this learning module, there are many readily accessible passages online for the chosen literary heroes (i.e., Sherlock Holmes, King Arthur, Nancy Drew, and Karana, from *Island of the Blue Dolphins*).

Doubling-Down with the Double Fishbone

Throughout Learning Module 5, gifted and advanced students will be introduced to the Double Fishbone (Mofield & Phelps, 2020; see Figure 4.2) as an evaluative processing model.

Figure 4.2 Double Fishbone.

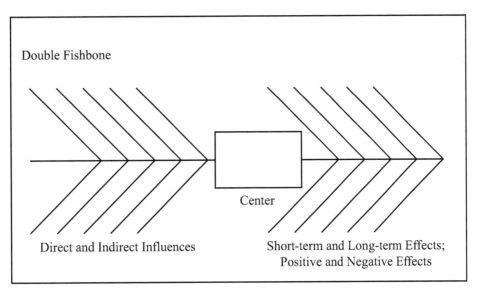

Double Fishbone

Center

Direct and Indirect Influences

Short-term and Long-term Effects;
Positive and Negative Effects

Source: From *Collaboration, Coteaching, and Coaching in Gifted Education: Sharing Strategies to Support Gifted Learners,* by E. Mofield & V. Phelps, 2020, Prufrock Press. Reprinted with permission of the authors.

By working through this strategy (adapted from Juntune, 2013), students typically identify a problem/issue, written in the center square, and then examine the causes which led to that problem on the lines to the left of the square, and the effects, or implications, of the problem on the lines to the right of the square.

For the context of this learning module, the Double Fishbone will be used to examine the challenges (e.g., society/systemic challenges, personal obstacles, family background) of each historical figure, written on the left side of the graphic organizer, as well as how the historical hero persevered to overcome the various obstacles, written on the right hand side of the graphic organizer. As students engage with this learning module, they will also apply the developed criteria from the first learning module to evaluate which historical hero exemplifies the most heroic qualities.

An online Double Fishbone to be utilized through Jamboard can be found at https://tinyurl.com/2e85th56. Remember to MAKE A COPY of the Jamboard before using with your own students.

Summary, Synthesis, and Selection

Students apply their established criteria throughout each learning module. As decisions are made regarding heroes that progress in the bracket challenge, students also align their decisions with real-world connections. These connections are made by incorporating the Future Problem Solvers (FPS; Torrance et al., 1977) categories. As part of this process, students relate how each identified hero, progressing to the next round, is most associated with the following categories:

- Arts and Aesthetics
- Basic Needs
- Business and Commerce
- Communication
- Defense
- Economics
- Education
- Environment
- Ethics and Religion
- Government and Politics
- Law and Justice
- Physical Health
- Psychological Health
- Recreation
- Social Relationships
- Technology
- Transportation

Similarly, in Learning Module 6, gifted and advanced learners will evaluate and justify which FPS categories are most closely aligned with the developed criteria. In doing so, students will be able to evaluate which of the final-bracket heroes are most closely associated with the developed, guiding criteria. Through this process, the evaluative process is guided by criterion-referenced evidence instead of personal bias. A reflection on the guiding question is also incorporated.

Ready for Lift-Off

With having a greater understanding of the different processing tools associated with each learning module, the following provides the "how-to" steps to create Learning Module 1 of this simulation. The same process could be followed to design new or alternate Google Forms simulations, as well. A link to the entire simulation (Learning Modules 1-6) can be accessed in the Support Material resources available at http://www.routledge.com/978164632213. After following the link, you will first need to MAKE A COPY of each learning module, and from your copies, you will be able to modify the learning modules as needed. Making a copy will also ensure that all student data are correctly directed to you.

If Google Forms is new to you, please refer to Tables 3.1 and 3.2 in Chapter 3 for an overview of the various tools and considerations of use for gifted and advanced learners. For the purpose of utilizing Google Forms for an online simulation, the importance of creating a theme cannot be understated. In regard to the ACES Astronaut Simulation, the rocket ship header works well (see Figure 4.3). In fact, it was the image of this header that actually inspired the theme for this entire simulation! Also, it will be important to set up your Google Forms simulation to collect email addresses prior to sharing the simulation with students.

The following section will provide the "how-to" information (see Tables 4.1 through Tables 4.5) to create Learning Module 1 of the ACES Astronaut Simulation. Each section of the simulation will include the needed steps of development and will be followed by a screenshot (see Figures 4.3 through 4.7) of what the corresponding section would look like in Google Forms. Images used as part of the simulation were designed by Freepik from www.freepik.com.

An Example of Practice: Learning Module 1

As the first learning module of the simulation, students are introduced to the overarching scenario of the online simulation and presented with the guiding question: *How does effective evaluation lead to stronger decision-making?* Throughout the course of this learning module, students are introduced to different types of heroes (e.g., superheroes, theatrical heroes, literary heroes, and historical heroes) and begin developing criteria and recognizing their impact on effective decision-making. Tables 4.1 through 4.5 provide the specific how-to details about creating Learning Module 1, while Figure 4.3 through 4.7 provide screenshots of the final simulation as viewed on Google Forms.

Table 4.1 Learning Module 1: Steps to Developing Section 1

Google Forms Icon	Google Forms Task	Text to Be Copied into Google Forms and Special Instructions
Step 1: Tт	Add Title and Description	**Type Title:** ACES Astronaut Training: Becoming an Advanced Criteria Evaluation Specialist (Module 1)
		Type Description: When you awoke this morning, it seemed like a perfectly normal day. You went through your typical morning routine of preparing for your school day, and nothing seemed out of the ordinary... that is... until there was a knock at the door. As you walked to the door, you could feel that something extraordinary was about to happen, but you just didn't quite know what. As you slowly turned the doorknob and peeked out of the door, you saw a strange man, standing there, dressed in a well-tailored suit. He promptly greeted you by name and invited you for a ride in the stretch limousine waiting on the street. Your family assured you that this is your destiny, so you decided to take him up on his offer.
		As you step into the limo, you find a note addressed to you. You quickly grab it and read the following:
		Greetings!
		You are among an elite group of scholars who have been selected for a top-secret mission as an ACES (Advanced Criteria Evaluation Specialist) Astronaut. To ensure your safety for this adventure, you must first complete a series of training exercises. You are currently en route to the ACES Astronaut Academy. As you enter the training facility, please proceed directly to the ACES Registration Desk and provide your name. In order to confirm that you are

(Continued)

Table 4.1 (Continued)

Google Forms Icon	Google Forms Task	Text to Be Copied into Google Forms and Special Instructions
		the correct recipient of the letter, you will also be prompted to create a random statement including the name of an animal (either real or imaginary). Your statement must also include the word "animal"… further instructions await.
Step 2: ⊕	Add Question	**Type Question:** Please enter the first and last name that you would like on your ACES identification badge. (You can have fun and be creative if you like or feel free to use your real name.)
		*Special Note: ♦ Select "Short answer" from the top drop-down menu. ♦ Select "Required" at bottom, right-hand corner.
🖾	Add Image	*** Special Note:** ♦ Search for a "fun" picture to signify an I.D. Badge or Name Tag and insert into this question space. This will help bring a little more "personality" to the simulation (see Figure 4.3).
Step 3: ⊕	Add Question	**Type Question:** To gain final clearance for ACES training, please complete the last task mentioned in your ACES letter. Upon completion of this final clearance question, you will be transported to your first training task.

		*Special Note:
		♦ Select "Paragraph" from the top drop-down menu.
		♦ Select "Required" at bottom, right-hand corner.
		♦ Click on three stacked dots at bottom, right-hand corner.
		  • Select "Regular Expression"
		  • Select "Contains"

(Continued)

Table 4.1 (Continued)

Google Forms Icon	Google Forms Task	Text to Be Copied into Google Forms and Special Instructions
		• Type the word "animal" • Type "ACES is looking forward to beginning your training. Please double check the directions included in your letter."
	Add Image	* **Special Note:** ♦ Search for a "fun" picture to signify the astronaut theme (e.g., astronaut and rocket ship)
Step 4:	Add Section	* **Special Note:** By clicking on "Add Section" a new section will be created for the next portion of the learning module. Students will *not* be able to proceed until all questions are answered in this section.

A Successful Launch

After each learning module throughout this simulation, the facilitating teacher will need to tabulate the "voting" results for each of the hero brackets to determine and announce to the class which hero is moving forward in the bracket challenge. Be mindful not to share the next learning module until students have been notified of which hero has progressed to the next round of the tournament. It will also be important to tally the associated FPS categories that students connect with each hero that progresses to the next round, as they will be using these categories as part of the evaluative thinking process in Learning Module 6.

Feel free to modify, adapt, and add to any parts of the provided simulation once making your own copy. This is a wonderful opportunity to integrate students' interests, as well. Also, while working in a blended learning environment, it is easy to provide students with hardcopies of the various materials if the simulation needs to be split between online and in-person instruction. Likewise, in knowing your particular group of students, feel free to find additional reading passages and research support documents to share with students.

Through several years of working through this challenge, it never ceases to amaze me the level of "buy-in" that students have in this process. Once you see this level of engagement from your gifted and advanced students, continue to challenge yourself to create new simulations based-off of your students' own interests and value systems. Find new ways to keep online learning fresh and innovative.

Figure 4.3 Learning Module 1: Section 2 Google Forms Visual.

ACES Astronaut Training: Becoming an Advanced Criteria Evaluation Specialist (Learning Module 1)

When you awoke this morning, it seemed like a perfectly normal day. You went through your typical morning routine of preparing for your school day, and nothing seemed out of the ordinary....that is...until there was a knock at the door. As you walked to the door, you could feel that something extraordinary was about to happen, but you just didn't quite know what. As you slowly turned the doorknob and peeked out of the door, you saw a strange man, standing there, dressed in a well-tailored suit. He promptly greeted you by name and invited you for a ride in the stretch limousine waiting on the street. Your family assured you that this is your destiny, so you decided to take him up on his offer.

As you step into the limo, you find a note addressed to you. You quickly grab it and read the following:

Greetings!
You are among an elite group of scholars who have been selected for a top-secret mission as an ACES (Advanced Criteria Evaluation Specialist) Astronaut. To ensure your safety for this adventure, you must first complete a series of training exercises. You are currently en route to the ACES Astronaut Academy. As you enter the training facility, please proceed directly to the ACES Registration Desk and provide your name. In order to confirm that you are the correct recipient of the letter, you will also be prompted to create a random statement including the name of an animal (either real or imaginary). Your statement must also include the word 'animal'...further instructions await.

*Required

Figure 4.3   (Continued)

Email*

Your email

Please enter the first and last name that you would like on your ACES identification badge. (You can have fun and be creative if you like or feel free to use your real name.)*

Your answer

To gain final clearance for ACES training. please complete the last task mentioned in your ACES letter.*

Your answer

Next

Table 4.2 Learning Module 1: Steps to Developing Section 2

Google Forms Icon	Google Forms Task	Text to Be Copied into Google Forms and Special Instructions (as Noted)
Step 1: **T**T	Add Title and Description	**Type Title:** Guiding Question: How does effective evaluation lead to stronger decision-making?
		Type Description: Welcome to your Level 1 training activity at ACES Astronaut Academy, where we pride ourselves on engaging our trainees through a variety of different tasks and exercises. To ensure that all of our graduates are fully prepared for their final destination, we ask that you take your training seriously and truly put forth your best effort. By doing so, you not only will be added to our long list of satisfied alumni, you will also feel more prepared for your future intergalactic missions. As part of our ongoing customer service, ACES Astronaut Academy will also be providing personalized feedback to your responses upon completion of this learning module before you proceed to your next level of training.
		To successfully complete this first level of training, please read through the following and complete the required questions. Once you have successfully completed this section, you will be advanced to the next level within this training module. We are hoping this Level 1 training provides you with an "out-of-this-world" experience!
Step 2: **T**T	Add Title and Description	**Type Title:** Task 1
		Type Description: As part of your ACES training, it is of great importance that you

(Continued)

Table 4.2 (Continued)

Google Forms Icon	Google Forms Task	Text to Be Copied into Google Forms and Special Instructions (as Noted)
		support the reasoning behind your thinking. ACES Astronaut Academy has worked diligently to provide you with all of the needed information to complete these tasks, and remember, an Aces Astronaut Academy Facilitator will be providing feedback to your responses upon completion of this module.
		For your first training task in becoming an ACES (Advanced Criteria Evaluation Specialist) Astronaut, you will be asked to consider the characteristics of a great hero. At this time, we request that you begin to work through the tasks that follow.
Step 3:	Add Image	**Image Title:** WHO IS THE GREATEST HERO?
		*Special Note: ♦ Prior to uploading this image, a table will need to be created and saved as a JPEG which includes the names and/or corresponding pictures of the heroes who are being referenced throughout this simulation (see Figure 4.4).
Step 4:	Add Question	**Type Question:** If you had to choose only one person or character from above, who would you select to be the greatest hero? In a paragraph, state who you would choose, and provide AT LEAST three supports to justify your reasoning.
		*Special Note: ♦ Select "Paragraph" from the top drop-down menu. Select "Required" at bottom, right-hand corner.

(Continued)

Table 4.2 (Continued)

Google Forms Icon	Google Forms Task	Text to Be Copied into Google Forms and Special Instructions (as Noted)
Step 5: ⊕	Add Question	**Type Question:** Take a moment to re-read your response to the previous question. Once you feel as though your answer provides a strong argument for why your selection is the greatest hero, please type the words BLAST OFF to be transported to your next task. (Make sure that you type them in capital letters!)

		*Special Note:
		♦ Select "Short answer" from the top drop-down menu.
		♦ Select "Required" at bottom, right-hand corner.
		♦ Click on three stacked dots at bottom, right-hand corner.
		  • Select "Text"
		  • Select "Contains"
		  • Type the words "BLAST OFF"
		  • Type "ACES Astronaut Academy can tell that you are close. Try again. We KNOW you can do it!"

🖼	Add Image	*** Special Note:** ♦ Search for a "fun" picture to signify the astronaut theme (e.g., astronaut and rocket ship)
Step 6: ▭▭	Add Section	*** Special Note:** By clicking on "Add Section" a new section will be created for the next portion of the learning module. Students will not be able to proceed until all questions are answered in this section.

Figure 4.4 Learning Module 1: Section 5 Google Forms Visual.

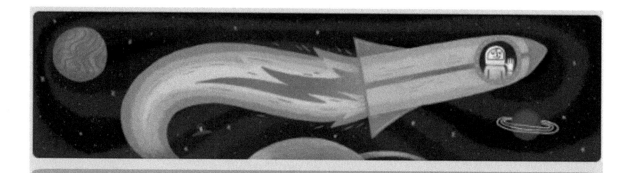

ACES Astronaut Training: Becoming an Advanced Criteria Evaluation Specialist (Learning Module 1)

* Required

Guiding Question: How does effective evaluation lead to stronger decision-making?

Welcome to your level 1 training activity at ACES Astronaut Academy, where we pride ourselves on engaging our trainees through a variety of different tasks and exercises. To ensure that all of our graduates are fully prepared for their final destination, we ask that you take your training seriously and truly put forth your best effort. By doing so, you not only will be added to our long list of satisfied alumni, you will also feel more prepared for your future intergalactic missions. As part of our ongoing customer service, ACES Astronaut Academy will also be providing personalized feedback to your responses upon completion of this learning module before you proceed to your next level of training.

To successfully complete this first level of training, please read through the following, and complete the required questions. Once you have successfully completed this section, you will be advanced to the next level within this training module. We are hoping this Level 1 training provides you with an 'out-of-this-world' experience!

Task 1

As part of your ACES training, it is of great importance that you support the reasoning behind your thinking. ACES Astronaut Academy has worked diligently to provide you with all of the needed information to complete these tasks, and remember, an Aces Astronaut Academy Facilitator will be providing feedback to your responses upon completion of this module.

For your first training tasks in becoming an ACES (Advanced Criteria Evaluation Specialist) Astronaut, you will be asked to consider the characteristics of a great hero. At this time, we request that you begin to work through the tasks that follow.

Figure 4.4 ((Continued)

WHO IS THE GREATEST HERO?

Black Panther	Spiderman	Wonder Woman	Superman
Abraham Lincoln	Sacagawea	Dr. Martin Luther King, Jr.	Albert Einstein
Yoda	Harry Potter	Maria Figueroa	Captain Kirk
Sherlock Holmes	King Arthur	Nancy Drew	Karana

If you had to choose only one person or character from above, who would you select to be the greatest hero? In a paragraph, state who you would choose, and provide AT LEAST three supports to justify your reasoning. *

Your answer

Take a moment to re-read your response to the previous question. Once you feel as though your answer provides a strong argument for why your selection is the greatest hero, please type the words BLAST OFF to be transported to your next task. (Make sure that you type them in capital letters!) *

Your answer

Back   Next

Figure 4.4 ((Continued)

Table 4.3 Learning Module 1: Steps to Developing Section 3

Google Forms Icon	Google Forms Task	Text to Be Copied into Google Forms and Special Instructions
Step 1: **T**t	Add Title and Description	**Type Title:** Guiding Question: How does effective evaluation lead to stronger decision-making?
Tt	Add Title and Description	**Type Description:** Was it really fair for Task 1 to ask you who the greatest hero was? Did you REALLY know enough about all of those people and characters to make a well-informed decision? In Task 2, reflect upon HOW you made your decision. Take some time to process your decision, and think through how you made your selection.
Step 2: 🖼	Add Image	**Image Title:** Here is a quick reminder of the available choices:
		*Special Note: ♦ Use the same image as in Step 3 of Section 2 above (see Figure 4.4).
Step 3: ⊕	Add Question	**Type Question:** Task 2: Write a reflective paragraph taking into consideration the following questions: HOW did you choose the greatest hero in Task 1? How do you define the word, hero? Might your decision be different if you had more information? Was your decision based on your own personal experience and knowledge of the people and characters? Explain your reasoning through this written reflection.
		*Special Note: ♦ Select "Paragraph" from the top drop-down menu. ♦ Select "Required" at bottom, right-hand corner.
🖼	Add Image	*** Special Note:** ♦ Search for a "fun" picture to signify the astronaut theme (e.g., astronaut and rocket ship)
Step 4: ▭▭	Add Section	*** Special Note:** By clicking on "Add Section" a new section will be created for the next portion of the Learning Module. Students will not be able to proceed until all questions are answered in this section.

Figure 4.5 Learning Module 1: Section 1 Google Forms Visual.

ACES Astronaut Training: Becoming an Advanced Criteria Evaluation Specialist (Learning Module 1)

* Required

Guiding Question: How does effective evalution lead to stronger decision-making?

Was it really fair for Task 1 to ask you who the greatest hero was? Did you REALLY know about all of those people and characters to make a well-informed decision? In Task 2, reflect upon HOW you made your decision. Take some time to process your decision, and think through how you made your selection.

Figure 4.5 (Continued)

Here is a quick reminder of the available choices:

Black Panther	Spiderman	Wonder Woman	Superman
Abraham Lincoln	Sacagawea	Dr. Martin Luther King, Jr.	Albert Einstein
Yoda	Harry Potter	Maria Figueroa	Captain Kirk
Sherlock Holmes	King Arthur	Nancy Drew	Karana

Task 2: Write a reflective paragraph taking into consideration the following questions: HOW did you choose the greatest hero in Task 1? How do you define the word, hero? Might your decision be different if you had more information? Was your decision based on your own personal experience and knowledge of the people and characters? Explain your reasoning through this written reflection. *

Your answer

Back   Next

Table 4.4 Learning Module 1: Steps to Developing Section 4

Google Forms Icon	Google Forms Task	Text to Be Copied into Google Forms and Special Instructions
Step 1:	Add Title and Description	**Type Title:** Well done, ACES Trainee!
		Type Description: For your next phase of training, you will be learning more about how understanding criteria can help you answer the Guiding Question: How does effective evaluation lead to stronger decision-making?
Step 2:	Add Title and Description	**Type Title:** How can we make our evaluative decisions even stronger?
		Type Description: Many times, people make decisions based on their emotions or because their friends are asking them to. Often, those types of decisions are not the best for the long term. Strong decision-making is the result of researching to make informed, evaluated decisions. For example, here at ACES Astronaut Academy, it is important that we develop safe rocket ships for our intergalactic travel. If we made our decisions based solely on which rockets were the prettiest, then we would be placing many of our astronauts' lives in danger. Instead, we take the time to learn more about the safety of the rocket, the cost of manufacturing the rocket, the needed fuel it requires, and other various considerations. All of these different categories help to create what we call CRITERIA!
Step 3:	Add Title and Description	**Type Title:** What are criteria, and how do I use them?
		Type Description: Criteria are defined as principles or standards by which something may be judged or decided. Criteria should

(Continued)

Table 4.4 (Continued)

Google Forms Icon	Google Forms Task	Text to Be Copied into Google Forms and Special Instructions
		also be written in "superlative" form. That means that criteria statements should include adverbs or adjectives that express the degree or extent of something. For example, superlatives might include: tallest, most challenging, friendliest, most helpful, best, etc…
		In using the above example of determining the best rocket ship to build, it is helpful to begin with writing a "best" statement. In this case, the statement might be, "The best rocket ship for use at ACES Astronaut Academy provides safety for our astronauts, is economical to manufacture, requires minimum fuel for successful blast-off, and incorporates the highest levels of technology available."
		From this generated statement, it becomes much easier to write appropriate criteria. In this example, the criteria for selecting the best rocket ship might include:
		*Which rocket is the SAFEST for astronauts?
		*Which rocket is the MOST economical to build?
		*Which rocket requires the LEAST amount of fuel?
		*Which rocket is the MOST technologically advanced?
		By creating and using criteria, the decision-making process becomes more evaluative and provides an opportunity to show "proof" for why a decision should be made instead of relying solely on feelings. As part

(Continued)

Table 4.4 (Continued)

Google Forms Icon	Google Forms Task	Text to Be Copied into Google Forms and Special Instructions
		of your ACES training, your next task will involve writing criteria to determine the best hero.
Step 4: ⊕	Add Question	**Type Question:** Task 3: Before you create your "hero" criteria, begin by writing 1–2 sentences, defining the characteristics of a hero. You could begin with, "A hero is someone who ____" (Make sure that you include multiple characteristics.)
		*Special Note: ♦ Select "Paragraph" from the top drop-down menu. ♦ Select "Required" at bottom, right-hand corner.
🖼	Add Image	*** Special Note:** ♦ Search for a "fun" picture to signify the astronaut theme (e.g., astronaut and rocket ship).
Step 5: ⊕	Add Question	**Type Question:** Now, take a look at what you just wrote and create AT LEAST 5 criteria for being The Greatest Hero. Look back at the rocket examples if you need to, and remember to use superlatives! (When you are done, MAKE SURE to write down your criteria somewhere else for future reference. This could be in a notebook or in an online document.)
		*Special Note: ♦ Select "Paragraph" from the top drop-down menu. ♦ Select "Required" at bottom, right-hand corner.

(Continued)

Table 4.4 (Continued)

Google Forms Icon	Google Forms Task	Text to Be Copied into Google Forms and Special Instructions
Step 6: **Tᴛ**	Add Title and Description	**Type Title:** For Task 4, take some time to think about what you have learned about criteria and answer the following question.
		*Special Note: No Description Needed
Step 7: ⊕	Add Question	**Type Question:** Task 4: How does creating criteria lead to effective evaluation and stronger decision-making skills? Please include how you might be able to use criteria in your own life. (As you respond in paragraph form, remember to think about meaningful word choice, appropriate punctuation, and sentence fluency.)
		*Special Note: ♦ Select "Paragraph" from the top drop-down menu. ♦ Select "Required" at bottom, right-hand corner.
▣	Add Image	*** Special Note:** ♦ Search for a "fun" picture to signify the astronaut theme (e.g., astronaut and rocket ship).
Step 8: ▤	Add Section	*** Special Note:** By clicking on "Add Section" a new section will be created for the next portion of the learning module. Students will not be able to proceed until all questions are answered in this section.

Figure 4.6 Learning Module 1: Section 4 Google Forms Visual.

ACES Astronaut Training: Becoming an Advanced Criteria Evaluation Specialist (Learning Module 1)

* Required

Well done, ACES Trainee!

For your next phase of training, you will be learning more about how understanding criteria can help you answer the Guiding Question: How does effective evalution lead to stronger decision-making?

How can we make our evaluative decisions even stronger?

Many times, people make decisions based on their emotions or because their friends are asking them to. Often, those types of decisions are not the best for the long term. Strong decision-making is the result of researching to make informed, evaluated decisions. For example, here at ACES Astronaut Academy, it is important that we develop safe rocket ships for our intergalactic travel. If we made our decisions based solely on which rockets were the prettiest, then we would be placing many of our astronauts lives in danger. Instead, we take the time to learn more about the safety of the rocket, the cost of manufacturing the rocket, the needed fuel it requires, and other various considerations. All of these different categories help to create what we call CRITERIA!

Figure 4.6   (Continued)

What are criteria, and how do I use them?

Criteria are defined as principles or standards by which something may be judged or decided. Criteria should also be written in 'superlative' form. That means that criteria statements should include adverbs or adjectives that express the degree or extent of something. For example, superlatives might include: tallest, most challenging, friendliest, most helpful, best, etc...

In using the above example of determining the best rocket ship to build, it is helpful to begin with writing a 'best' statement. In this case, the statement might be, 'The best rocket ship for use at ACES Astronaut Academy provides safety for our astronauts, is economical to manufacture, requires minimum fuel for successful blast-off, and incorporates the highest levels of technology available.'

From this generated statement, it becomes much easier to write appropriate criteria. In this example, the criteria for selecting the best rocket ship might include:

*Which rocket is the SAFEST for astronauts?
*Which rocket is the MOST economical to build?
*Which rocket requires the LEAST amount of fuel?
*Which rocket is the MOST technologically advanced?

By creating and using criteria, the decision-making process becomes more evaluative and provides an opportunity to show 'proof' for why a decision should be made instead of relying solely on feelings. As part of your ACES training, your next task will involve writing criteria to determine the best hero.

Task 3: Before you create your 'hero' criteria, begin by writing 1-2 sentences, defining the characteristics of a hero. You could begin with, "A hero is someone who....." (Make sure that you include multiple characteristics.) *

Your answer
_____

Figure 4.6 (Continued)

Now, take a look at what you just wrote and create AT LEAST 5 criteria for being The Greatest Hero. Look back at the rocket examples if you need to, and remember to use superlatives! (when you are done, MAKE SURE to write down your criteria somewhere else for future reference. This could be in a notebook or in an online document.) *

Your answer

For Task 4, take some time to think about what you have learned about criteria and answer the following question.

Task 4: How does creating criteria lead to effective evaluation and stronger decision-making skills? Please include how you might be able to use criteria in your own life. (As you respond in paragraph form, remember to think about meaningful word choice, appropriate punctuation, and sentence fluency.) *

Your answer

Back   Next

Table 4.5 Learning Module 1: Steps to Developing Section 5

Google Forms Icon	Google Forms Task	Text to Be Copied into Google Forms and Special Instructions
Step 1: **Tᴛ**	Add Title and Description	**Type Title:** Well done, ACES Trainee! You have just completed Module 1 of your ACES training.
		Type Description: Creating criteria is definitely a first step in using effective evaluation for stronger decision-making skills, but without knowing anything more about many of the heroes that were presented at the beginning of this learning module, it would be very difficult to use the criteria in a meaningful manner. THAT is why we are preparing you to engage in the first ever ACES HERO-BRACKET CHAMPIONSHIP!
		Over the course of the next few learning modules, your ACES training will take you on an adventure to narrow down the candidates to the ULTIMATE HERO OF ALL TIME! For the purposes of your training, the heroes will be divided into 4 Hero Brackets, consisting of Superheroes, Theatrical Heroes, Literary Heroes, and Historical Heroes.
		Each learning module will present you with a new critical thinking model which will help you make some very difficult decisions in moving forward. Your decisions, along with the decisions of your fellow ACES trainees, will determine which hero will progress to the next challenge. It is up to you, ACES trainee, to proceed with Module 2 to determine which Superhero will survive to challenge another hero!
Step 2: ⊕	Add Question	**Type Question:** As your final task for Module 1, please rate your level of understanding of creating criteria. (We will be applying these criteria our heroes in later Modules.) When you are done, make sure to click the "Submit" button below.
		*Special Note: ♦ Select "Linear scale" from the top drop-down menu.

(Continued)

Table 4.5 (Continued)

Google Forms Icon	Google Forms Task	Text to Be Copied into Google Forms and Special Instructions
		• Level 1: Type "I feel very confused about criteria." • Level 5: Type "I am a hero at understanding criteria!" ♦ Select "Required" at bottom, right-hand corner.

Figure 4.7 Learning Module 1: Section 3 Google Forms Visual.

ACES Astronaut Training: Becoming an Advanced Criteria Evaluation Specialist (Learning Module 1)

* Required

Well done, ACES Trainee! You have just completed Module 1 of your ACES training.

Creating criteria is definitely a first step in using effective evaluation for stronger decision-making skills, but without knowing anything more about many of the heroes that were presented at the beginning of this learning module, it would be very difficult to use the criteria in a meaningful manner. THAT is why we are preparing you to engage in the first ever ACES HERO-BRACKET CHAMPIONSHIP!

Over the course of the next few learning modules, your ACES training will take you on an adventure to narrow down the candidates to the ULTIMATE HERO OF ALL TIME! FOR the purposes of your training, the heroes will be divided into 4 Hero Brackets, consisting of Superheroes, Theatrical Heroes, Literary Heroes, and Historical Heroes.

Each learning module will present you with a new critical thinking model which will help you make some very difficult decisions in moving forward. Your decisions, along with the decisions of your fellow ACES trainees, will determine which hero will progress to the next challenge. It is up to you, ACES trainee, to proceed with Module 2 to determine which Superhero will survive to challenge another hero!

Figure 4.7 (Continued)

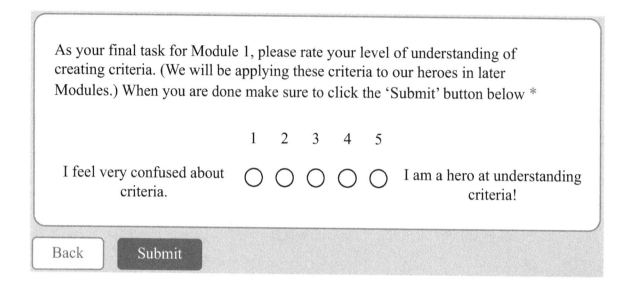

As your final task for Module 1, please rate your level of understanding of creating criteria. (We will be applying these criteria to our heroes in later Modules.) When you are done make sure to click the 'Submit' button below *

As a reminder, directions to access the remaining learning modules associated with the ACES Astronaut Simulation can be easily accessed at www.routledge.com/ 9781646322213 and will provide students the opportunity to work through:

◆ Learning Module 2: Concept Mapping as a Problem-Solving Tool (Focus: Superheroes)
◆ Learning Module 3: Elements of Reasoning (Focus: Theatrical Heroes)
◆ Learning Module 4: Analytical Thinking (Focus: Literary Heroes)
◆ Learning Module 5: Double Fishbone (Focus: Historical Heroes)
◆ Learning Module 6: The Winner Is…

Also remain mindful of providing ongoing feedback throughout the entire simulation experience (see Chapter 3).

Chapter 5

Google Sites as a Long-Term Engagement Strategy

In the field of education, Google Sites is commonly used as a class webpage to share information with parents and students about what is going on in the classroom, upcoming activities, and examples of student work. This is a wonderful tool for this purpose, but Google Sites also provides an incredible opportunity to create an engaging venue for online and blended learning. This chapter provides an overview of how to use Google Sites as a portal for learning through an online simulation for Soldiers of A.L.I.V.E. (American Legions Investigating Virtual Explorations). In addition to providing an overview of the various features of this simulation, this chapter also provides a link for you to upload your own assignments and projects to the Soldiers of A.L.I.V.E. Headquarters simulation site to use with your own blended and/or online distance classroom.

For those not familiar with online simulations within the classroom, imagine a site where students are able to log in, be immersed in a storyline where they are an integral character, and are provided with the opportunity to work through a series of assignments, projects, and various learning experiences while working to earn experience points (XP), badges, and items through both collaborative and autonomous approaches to learning.

In regard to online simulations developed to meet the unique learning needs of gifted and advanced learners, the associated learning tasks create additional opportunities to think deeply and critically about topics of study, as well as an opportunity to extend learning beyond the typical scope and sequence often provided by textbooks and school districts. While Chapter 4 provided an overview for simulations through Google Forms, this chapter focuses on how to create online simulations that span a greater length of time, including simulations that last the length of one unit of study or for the entire school year. The decision is totally up to you!

Simulation Sites

With the ongoing quest to engage gifted and advanced learners through challenging and complex online learning experiences, a continued focus on actively involving students is paramount. Gifted and advanced learners simply are not satisfied with passive

DOI: 10.4324/9781003238317-5

memorization and regurgitation of surface level knowledge (Trna, 2014), and as such, their online learning experiences should present opportunities to ignite curiosity, problem-solve, and make abstract connections to their conceptual understanding.

Active involvement in the learning process also sustains gifted and advanced learners' interest for extended periods of time (Renninger & Hindi, 2011), and online simulations are one instructional approach which provides gifted and advanced learners with both autonomous and collaborative opportunities, as well as what many consider to be an immersive experience. While there are online, content-specific simulations available (e.g., dissections, virtual field trips), creating an academically focused simulation to address key learning objectives and standards allows gifted and advanced learners the opportunity to explore rigorous content and advance their learning in new and exciting ways (Siegle, 2019) that ultimately lead students to moments of discovery (Donally, 2019).

First Things First

In addition to being able to integrate a variety of applications into Google Sites, there are a few key components to understand when creating your own simulation site or adding to the Soldiers of A.L.I.V.E. simulation portal (link provided later in chapter). Table 5.1 provides a quick reference of the various options/tools readily available on Google Sites.

The Soldiers of A.L.I.V.E. simulation portal serves *only* as a portal through which all subject-specific content for gifted and advanced students will need to be uploaded. This is accomplished by creating an additional content specific assignment or Google Site which will be hyperlinked into the Soldiers of A.L.I.V.E. Time Travel Continuum (see below). While it might initially sound a little overwhelming, it is really no different than uploading documents into your regular learning management system (e.g., Google Classroom, Canvas, Blackboard) for students to access and complete. Continue to reference Table 5.1 as needed. More information on integration of content will be discussed later in this chapter.

Establishing Purpose, Structure, and Clear Expectations

As with any meaningful learning experience, simulations need to have purpose, structure, and well-communicated expectations to ensure that students are able to successfully navigate and achieve the desired outcomes of the simulation. More specifically, for gifted and advanced learners, the simulation needs to encapsulate learning opportunities that advance the content, build the buy-in, and create a challenge (Mofield, 2019; Mofield & Phelps, 2020). This continues to stress the importance of creating simulations that address the unique learning needs of gifted and advanced learners.

By using an online simulation to meet these needs, it is helpful to have a foundation of anchors, or structure, to help guide students as they progress through the various learning experiences. Table 5.2 provides an overview of the key game terms as used as part of the Soldiers of A.L.I.V.E. simulation. These terms are also provided as part of the students' Soldiers of A.L.I.V.E. Handbook (see end of chapter). By providing students with this reference of key game terms, they are better prepared to successfully navigate the simulation experience. As an added bonus, the process of building the context for the simulation continues to create more excitement and intrigue as students eagerly anticipate the start of the simulation.

Expectations are further established through the structure of the simulation, itself. This is done primarily by incorporating a set of clearly communicated bylaws, as well as badges,

Table 5.1 Basic Overview of Google Sites Icons/Tools

Icon	Task	How to Use
T_T	Insert Text	◆ Add or insert text to title pages, type-in the story-line for your students' simulation, provide instructions, etc. Basically, anytime you would like to type, this is the icon for you!
🖼	Add Image	◆ Add images to enhance the simulation experience. This will help students feel like they are actually part of the game.
< >	Embed Link	◆ By embedding links, students are able to click on a picture, a title, or any other focus item and be transported (through the embedded link) to another Google Site, virtual experience, or URL that contributes to the online student learning experience. Consider integrating virtual exploration links to immerse your students in the ability to navigate learning through a 360° experience. See Chapter 6 for suggested links.
▲	Google Drive	◆ This helpful link allows you to have "quick click" access to any Google Documents, Forms, Slides, etc. that you would like to upload or integrate with your Google Site. Do not feel like you have to recreate the wheel. Upload your tried and true learning activities as part of your simulation.
☁	Upload File	◆ Upload any assignment, example, image, etc. that you already have saved to your computer into your Google Site to continue to add to a student's learning experience. Remember to keep the learning focused on advanced content, advanced processing tools, and a connection to abstract, conceptual understandings.
▭	Create Button	◆ This is a nice option if you are looking to create a "push button" for students. In essence, the button will be embedded with a link of your choosing.
▱	Student View	◆ As you create or continue to enhance your Google Site, it is very helpful to see what it looks like from the student perspective. Click on this icon at the top of your Google Sites page to gain this perspective.

Table 5.2 Soldiers of A.L.I.V.E. Game Terms

Avatar	An in-game image for a student. It represents the virtual persona of the student as a Soldier of A.L.I.V.E.
Battalion	One of the smaller assigned groups found within a bunker (class). Students will work closely with this collaborative group through small group activities.
Battle Points	These are points that are found on many items. Battle Points help students during battles (e.g., a class review game, challenges). These points do NOT add to a student's academic score, but they may add to the student's overall XP.
Bunker	The entire class period is referred to as a bunker. Within each bunker, there will be other military divisions. For an elementary teacher, there might only be one bunker, but for a secondary teacher, there could be multiple bunkers based on the different class periods being taught.
Craft	The act of constructing something. This could include a writing project or various other creative projects.
Division	One of the smaller assigned groups found within a bunker (class). Students will work closely with this collaborative group through small group activities.
Item	Items are earned and may be used throughout the simulation to help on various tasks or to make a student's life a little bit easier or more enjoyable. Students should use these items wisely.
Leader Badge	Any badge with LB in the corner counts for the required passport to the "A" range for a graded course. Leader Badges signify required coursework and should be developed to meet the desired learning outcomes for a unit of study. For example, in a World War I unit of study, there might be a Leadership Badge for an activity focused on the Treaty of Versailles. Students should be encouraged to seek out as many of these as possible, as they carry a high XP value.
Level of Honor	A level that signifies a student's level of play as based on current XP standings as determined by the classroom teacher. For example, Level 1 might be determined for students between 0-500 XP, Level 2 for students 501-1000 XP, and Level 3 1001 XP and above. These levels are predetermined and communicated by the teacher prior to starting the simulation.
Item Case	The location associated with where the student "houses" their earned items. This might include an online folder or a pocket folder with brads within a traditional classroom setting.

(Continued)

Table 5.2 (Continued)

Mini Badge	Any badge that is not an LB is a Mini Badge. These are earned for various challenges within the simulation and represent learning experiences that are worthwhile and meaningful but might not be directly tied to essential learnings from the unit of study. For example, in a World War I unit of study, there might be a Mini Badge for an activity focused on the controversy related to the sinking of the Lusitania. While these are not LB, they do help students continue to delve deeper into their conceptual understanding of a unit and provide a nice source of additional XP.
Platoon	One of the smaller assigned groups found within a bunker (class). Students will work closely with this collaborative group through small group activities.
Player/ Soldier	Another name for a student.
Quests	These are the center of A.L.I.V.E. soldier training. Quests are optional activities for students to partake in to earn additional XP, items, and the very best Leader Badges. To succeed within the simulation, students must tackle many quests. Quests fall into three categories: ♦ **Solo Quest**: Quest that one must do alone. ♦ **Pick-up Quest**: Quest that requires a student to work with a group *outside* of their military group (e.g., battalion, division, platoon). ♦ **Military Quest**: Quest that is designed for a student's military group (e.g., battalion, division, platoon) and that group only.
XP	Experience Points that are earned by completing various quests throughout the simulation or compiled through earned items. Those who achieve the highest number of XP by the end of the simulation become 5-Star Generals.

XP, and other items that students can earn and strive for throughout each task (see following sections). As with any learning experience, the purpose behind the learning should also be clearly communicated and can be accomplished by sharing essential questions, learning objectives, and connections to the real world.

Bylaws of A.L.I.V.E.

For this simulation, the Bylaws of A.L.I.V.E. create the overarching expectations associated with navigating the simulation through the selected military theme (see Table 5.3) and are also included as part of the Soldiers of A.L.I.V.E Handbook (see end of chapter). While these are provided as an example, creating norms and expectations with gifted and advanced learners is always a meaningful experience, so please feel free to have your students become involved with creating and/or modifying these provided suggestions.

Table 5.3 Bylaws for Soldiers of A.L.I.V.E.

Bylaw	Guiding Principles
Bylaw 1: The Soldier's Honor Code	◆ Respect the process. ◆ Respect your peers. ◆ Respect yourself. ◆ Respect the work.
Bylaw 2: Leader Badges	◆ To earn an "A" each grading period, you must have earned a Leader Badge within that time frame (see Badges, Items, and XP section) ◆ An earned Leader Badge does NOT guarantee an "A" in the course. ◆ Do not procrastinate in earning Leader Badges. There are not endless opportunities.
Bylaw 3: Organizational Protocol	◆ All items must be stored in your Military Portfolio (see Badges, XP, and Items section). ◆ Only items that are currently stored in your Military Portfolio are able to be redeemed for use.
Bylaw 4: Honesty Pledge	◆ A.L.I.V.E. does not tolerate any cheating or unethical behavior. ◆ All judgments by The General are final.
Bylaw 5: Soldier Responsibilities	◆ Be personally responsible for your own work and behavior. ◆ Be a proactive problem-solver! ◆ All missions must be completed *before* the end of the unit.

Badges

Badges are the heart of A.L.I.V.E. and serve as an additional accountability measure within the simulation. As briefly referenced in Table 5.3, clear expectations should be set regarding how many badges must be earned in order to be successful within the class. For some classes, this might include an official grade; for other classes, it might include standards that students are working toward mastery. In any case, students should have a clear understanding for the purpose and process of earning badges.

In addition to serving as an additional means for the teacher to measure student progress, badges also provide gifted and advanced learners with an opportunity to further develop integral psychosocial skills focused on goal setting, time management, perseverance, and reflection on learning. As such, there are three different types of badges:

- Level of Honor Badge
- Leader Badge
- Mini Badge

Figure 5.1 Examples of Level of Honor Badges: Soldiers of A.L.I.V.E.

(a)
(b)

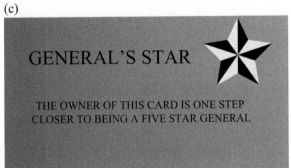

(c)

The Level of Honor Badge

This type of badge provides students with a clear understanding of the "level" that they are working in throughout the simulation (see Figure 5.1). All students begin the simulation at Level 1, and as they progress in their learning and gain additional XP, they also progress to higher levels of play. As students reach higher levels of XP, they have greater access to different activities and are able to redeem a greater number of earned items (see Items section). Online access to a sample of these badges can also be found at: https://docs.google.com/presentation/d/1YSf0k3UXpMA817r2MigMZZHZ5w_iVt90-Dw4AD3yT-0/edit?usp=sharing.

The Leader Badge

Leader Badges (see Figure 5.2) are difficult to earn and often include the greatest levels of depth and complexity. In many classrooms that include grades, Leader Badges are often a requirement for an "A" in a course, but simply having earned a Leader Badge does not equate to an automatic "A." Students should be highly encouraged to earn as many Leader Badges as possible, as they are focused heavily on key content from a unit of study and as such, carry high levels of XP. When planning a simulation, Leader Badges can become a requirement for a unit of study. All Leader Badges will be signified by an LB in the bottom right-hand corner.

The Mini Badge

Any badges that are NOT Leader Badges or Level of Honor Badges are considered Mini Badges (see Figure 5.3). This type of badge can be earned through a variety of different challenges within the simulation and typically include learning experiences that contribute to the understanding of the content but are not as integral to achieving the desired

Figure 5.2 Examples of Leader Badges: Soldiers of A.L.I.V.E.

(a)   (b)

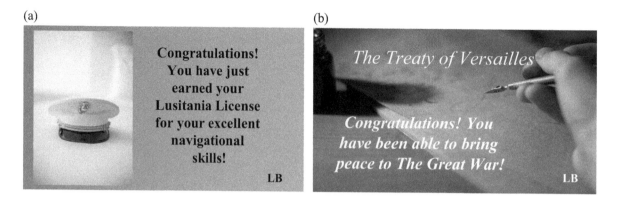

Figure 5.3 Example of Mini Badge: Soldiers of A.L.I.V.E.

outcomes. Mini Badges are excellent opportunities to integrate additional enrichment activities and challenges throughout the simulation. While Mini Badges are not a necessity in earning an "A" in a course, they are worth a great deal of XP, counting toward end game scoring, and as such, add an additional level of motivation to the simulation experience to work beyond what is typically expected within the classroom.

XP

As students progress through a simulation, XP, or Experience Points, provide a means for the students and teacher to measure progress through the various learning activities. As the creator of the simulation, the teacher is able to determine if XP will be based on the difficulty level of each task, the associated grade earned by completion of each task, as an added benefit of earned items (see next section), or a combination of any of these factors. If the decision is made to incorporate XP based off of the associated rewards with various learning tasks, one must remain mindful of the stigma that might be associated with low-scoring students. Because of this, it is highly recommended that XP *is not* based-off of the associated grades, alone. Resource 5 provides a planning sheet for designating a simulation's learning tasks with the associated rewards (i.e., XP, Items, Badges) for each task (see Figure 5.4). By preplanning the available learning tasks with associated rewards prior to implementing the simulation, the ongoing management of the learning experience is much easier.

Resource 5 Planning Sheet for Simulation Learning Tasks with Associated Rewards

Simulation Learning Unit: _____	
Learning Task	**Associated Rewards (XP, Items, Badges, etc)**

Figure 5.4 *Planning Sheet Example for Simulation Learning Tasks with Associated Rewards.*

Simulation Learning Unit: WWI Soldiers of A.L.I.V.E. Simulation Unit

Learning Task	Associated Rewards (XP, Items, Badges, etc)
Primary Source Documents: Uploaded reading material with embedded secret code (Uncle Sam)	25 XP + Item
Propaganda Quest	75 XP + Item
Foreign Policy Military Quest	100 XP + Mini Badge
Military Group WWI Map	1st Place = 30 XP 2nd Place = 20 XP 3rd Place = 10 XP
Trench Warfare Quest	50 XP + Item
Lusitania Quest	XP based on grade + 25 additional XP + Leadership Badge for anyone scoring above 85%.
Lusitania Debate	10 XP for every point given for winning argument
Peace Treaty	20 XP for every term included in Versailles strips AND 20 XP for top scoring military group overall
Completion of ALL Quests for WWI	Stripes Item and 250 XP

The use of XP further increases the motivation and buy-in of gifted and advanced learners. This is primarily because these points serve as an accountability factor with peers, but as an added bonus, XP also allow students to acquire items that will help them throughout the simulation experience (see next section). This is very similar to earning various items throughout the course of a video game that help the player reach the level of success they are seeking to achieve. Those who achieve the highest number of XP by the end of the simulation become Five Star Generals.

Figure 5.5 Examples of Items: Soldiers of A.L.I.V.E.

XP Leaderboard

To further increase student accountability, it is helpful to create an XP Leaderboard. This serves as an ongoing visual to help students see their current XP stats as compared with their peers. Students can use their real names or code names, but having an XP Leaderboard is much like having a "Game Master" hierarchy in a video game, where top players' scores are shown, and players put forth extra effort to see their name at the top of the leaderboard. An XP Leaderboard can be easily created through the free Leader Board template found at https://flippity.net/. This same display could be used within a traditional classroom setting and updated and posted on a regular basis to maintain the "game" feel of the simulation within the classroom. Another option is to use any spreadsheet (e.g., Excel, Google Sheets) and once the data is entered, create a bar graph to provide a visual representation of the leaderboard to be displayed within the online or traditional classroom setting.

Table 5.4 Suggested Rules for "Items" Earned within the Soldiers of A.L.I.V.E. Simulation

Rule 1	In order to use an item that has a level printed on it, you must have first earned that level in your military training.
Rule 2	All earned items must be housed in your military folder (see next section). If using a pocket-folder system within the classroom, items should not be stacked. Stacking means to place more than one item on top of another. However, two items may be placed in one pocket if they are facing different directions.
Rule 3	Items are allowed to be traded.
Rule 4	No refunds are given.
Rule 5	No replacements are given for lost items.
Rule 6	Only items that are visually present can be redeemed. You will not be allowed to use an item if it is not in your immediate possession.

Items

As participants in the simulation, students are provided with an opportunity to earn various "items" (see Figure 5.5) throughout their simulated learning experiences. These items not only help them in their ultimate quest of becoming a Five Star General, they also keep the simulation fun and interesting by providing some extra perks and rewards to the students. Online access to a sample of these items can also be found at: https://docs.google.com/presentation/d/1EnOFLHIljHSe9pGSjHDTWXlItJdrsW7_h5L8wYs9unY/edit?usp=sharing.

As with any successful simulation learning experience, it is important to communicate clear expectations on how items are earned and how they can be redeemed. This information should also be clearly communicated as part of the Soldiers of A.L.I.V.E. Handbook (see Resource 6). Table 5.4 provides an overview of suggested rules regarding earned "items" within the Soldiers of A.L.I.V.E. simulation experience.

Classroom Management Tips

Knowing how to manage an online simulation is also a key factor in successful implementation of long-term online simulations. First, one must consider if the simulation is being conducted through a complete distance learning model or through a blended learning model within a traditional classroom. Other considerations might include:

◆ Is the simulation a requirement for all students?
◆ Will the simulation provide additional learning opportunities that extend beyond the scope and sequence required by the class?
◆ How will the simulation be provided to students who do not have access to online learning from home?
◆ Is the simulation part of curriculum compacting as a means to provide new learning for a student who has demonstrated mastery of a unit of study?
◆ If used within a blended classroom setting, will all students have access to computers at the same time, or do students need to rotate through a select number of available computers?
◆ How will meaningful and purposeful feedback be provided to students throughout the simulation experience?

While these are just a few guiding questions, it is important to consider the purpose and desired outcomes of the simulation while planning to meet the needs of gifted and advanced learners. In addition, there are the logistics of the basic management and assessment of the simulation that must be considered as well. The following sections will provide a brief overview of various management techniques for use within the distance classroom setting (e.g., cloud-based) and the blended classroom setting (hardcopy-based). It should be noted that within a blended classroom setting, the distance management suggestions are also applicable. Likewise, in situations where distance learning is required (e.g., natural disaster, pandemic) but students do not have online access at home, the blended classroom suggestions are a viable option to maintain ongoing student involvement in the simulation. When establishing which management practices work best within your setting and personal style, make sure you take the time to focus on what management suggestion best suits your needs (e.g., focused on one unit of study, continued over the course of a semester, continued over the course of a school year).

Managing an Online Distance Classroom Simulation

While managing a Google Site simulation for an exclusively distance classroom, it is important to create a sustainable approach to managing student progress throughout the entire simulation. More specifically, consider how you, as the teacher, as well as your students, are able to easily view the available and earned badges and items, as well as current XP levels.

When dealing with badges and items, it is helpful to use an already established online tracking system such as flippity.net. With this type of application, it simply requires the input of student names, or code names, along with the names and associated images for each badge or item. From a management perspective, the online viewing capability is automatically updated as the teacher records that a student has earned a particular badge or item. If a teacher would like to create their own system, this could be achieved through the use of a spreadsheet (e.g., Excel, Google Sheets), or the teacher could create a separate online folder for each student where appropriate images could be copied to signify each earned badge or item.

How a student earns a badge is fairly straightforward, as each badge is directly associated with the completion of a learning task. Items, however, are a bit more ambiguous because the items received are more random in nature and not directly associated with any task. When managing which items are earned, a randomizer spinning wheel can be utilized (e.g., Randomizer Wheel at flippity.net) or a teacher could create a coded system, whether through online communication or through a choice board (see Chapter 6) where a student selects a certain number or letter and then receives the associated item. With either approach, the received item would be noted within the student's personal folder or as part of the Soldiers of A.L.I.V.E. Headquarters online tracker.

When working to manage students' various online XP levels, it is most helpful to use a spreadsheet. First, create a spreadsheet with all of the students' names and all available tasks with associated values for a unit of study. For example, all students' names could be listed in Column 1 of a spreadsheet. Then, each subsequent column would be titled with the task and associated XP for completion. As students complete the various tasks, the XP would be updated.

Managing a Blended Classroom Simulation

While using an online simulation through blended learning, the online management suggestions discussed above are always an available option. Often, however, students like to have something tangible to signify personal progress. Through integrating the online simulation through a blended classroom, this is a great option. After navigating online simulations over the years, learning folders have been found to be an inexpensive and simple method for storing and managing student progress. With this approach, each student is provided with their own gaming folder (i.e., pocket folder with brads).

Gaming folders can be housed within the classroom and provide a space for students to store their earned badges and items, as well as any "in progress" work. The folders with brads also make it easy to utilize 9-pocket plastic collector pages that are typically used for collecting baseball cards, Pokémon cards, or other similar collectables. These are easily found for a nominal cost and can be reused each year as a means to store earned badges and items. Gaming folders also continue to bridge the gap for students who may not have online access at home by providing a means to send home hardcopies of any online assignments associated with the gaming simulation.

Over the years, I have found it worth the initial time investment to create Level of Honor Badges and Item Cards utilizing a standard business card template, as included in any word processing application. Each card is created with an image, a title, and a short description of what it is (see Figure 5.1). These are then easily stored within the 9-pocket plastic collector pages. This also allows for students to easily trade Item Cards. While this is not a necessity, it is something that students look forward to and enjoy, and as an added benefit, it keeps them highly engaged in the gaming aspect of the online simulation. It is recommended to laminate the cards for durability and easy sanitation.

Likewise, using self-adhesive address labels for earned Leadership Badges and Mini Badges also works well. Most of these self-adhesive labels include an online template to create and print the desired label content. Larger address labels work well for Leadership Badges (see Figure 5.2), while smaller labels work well for Mini Badges (see Figure 5.3). As students earn badges, they look forward to affixing them to the front of their gaming folders.

In regard to earning Item Cards, the spinning randomizer wheel at flippity.net, as mentioned earlier, is always an option, but it also works just as well to have an Item Card grab bag that students reach into when they have qualified to receive an item. The students love the anticipation of what they will retrieve, and it also allows you, as the teacher, to have more control over the probability of receiving certain items.

Table 5.5 provides suggested online simulation management techniques that might be utilized through both distance and blended classroom settings.

Boot Camp for the Soldiers of A.L.I.V.E. Simulation

Thus far, this chapter has focused on the overview of how to establish and manage an online simulation through Google Sites. While this is important information, it has not yet specifically addressed how to address the needs of gifted and advanced learners. This will come through the integration of advanced content, advanced processing models, and abstract connections to learning as uploaded and managed through the Google Site.

Integrating Content

Whether you choose to incorporate the provided Soldiers of A.L.I.V.E. Headquarters' simulation site (https://sites.google.com/view/aliveheadquarters) into your classroom

Table 5.5 Online Simulation Management Techniques for Distance and Blended Classroom Settings

Management Task	Distance Classroom Setting (Cloud-based)	Blended Classroom Setting (Hard Copy-based)
Badges	Suggestions include: ♦ Flippity.net online Badge Tracker ♦ Creating personal online folders for each student to copy and paste selected images, representing earned badges	Suggestions include: ♦ Print badges on self-adhesive labels to affix to the front of gaming folders (i.e., pocket folders with brads)
Items	Random selection through: ♦ Spinning wheel randomizer (e.g., flippity.net) ♦ Letter/Number correlation with items on choice boards (i.e., each item is associated with a particular number or letter) Manage through: ♦ Online Badge Tracker (e.g., flippity.net)	Random selection through ♦ Letter/Number correlation selections (i.e., each item is associated with a particular number or letter) ♦ Grab bag (i.e., students reach into a bag to select a random item) Manage through ♦ Print items on "business card" templates ♦ Pocket folders with brads and 9-pocket plastic collector pages for storage
XP	Manage through: ♦ Online Leader Board (e.g., flippity.net and spreadsheet)	Manage through: ♦ Online Leader Board (e.g., flippity.net and spreadsheet)
Limited/No Online Access at Home	→	Manage through: ♦ Gaming folders (e.g., pocket folders with brads) ♦ Hard copy assignments

(see Figure 5.6) or decide to develop one of your own, you will also need to integrate advanced content and accompanying learning activities for student completion. As you are first starting out, consider incorporating activities and reading selections that you would typically use in a traditional classroom setting. For instance, if your students are learning about a historical time period, it would be helpful to upload primary sources, secondary sources, and learning activities that support the desired standards and learning objectives.

Figure 5.6 Soldiers of A.L.I.V.E. Headquarters Home Screen.

(a)

(b)

Welcome to Your Time-Travel Continuum

The year is 2870, and you are now an active member of A.L.I.V.E. (American Legions Investigating Virtual Explorations). It is your job, your mission, your life's goal to travel back in time to experience the crude and archaic history of the United States. Along the way, you will be faced with daily challenges, times of war, and economic hardships. As you begin each mission, this site will serve as your time-travel continuum to transport you to your next destination. Please make sure that you read and are familiar with the Soldiers of A.L.I.V.E. Handbook provided on this site. Thank you for your loyal and devoted service.

As students access the simulation site, they will see several things on the home screen for the Soldiers of A.L.I.V.E. Headquarters:

◆ **The Welcome Screen:** Provides an introduction to the simulation experience and provides the Time Travel Continuum, which will serve as the hyperlink transport to units of study.
◆ **Handbook:** Provides a basic overview of the simulation, as well as the BYLAWS of A.L.I.V.E. and information on Badges and Items/Supplies.
◆ **Soldier XP Levels:** Provides a space for student XP levels.
◆ **Commendations:** Provides a space for a quick overview of available badges and badges earned by each student.
◆ **Items/Supplies:** Provides a space for a quick overview of available items/supplies earned by each student.

By using the various options on the homepage, it is easy to upload any content to further challenge gifted and advanced learners. To do this, a separate hyperlink will need to be copied and pasted into the Time Travel Continuum image on the Soldiers of A.L.I.V.E. Homepage. As students click on the center of that image, they will be instantly transported, as a Soldier of A.L.I.V.E., to their next destination. One of the easiest ways to accomplish this is to create a new Google Site link which assignments can easily be uploaded to. Along with uploading the specific tasks for student completion, it also provides an opportunity to continue to build upon the Soldiers of A.L.I.V.E. storyline. Have fun with it! Often, it works well to create a new Google Site link for each different unit of study when incorporating the simulation over the course of a year. For example, for a social studies course focused on United States History, separate sites/units of focus might include The Civil War and Reconstruction, The Progressive Era, The Roaring 20s, World War I, The Great Depression, and World War II.

Regardless of the content, a continued focus on creating learning tasks that continue to challenge and engage gifted and advanced learners is paramount. Seek out opportunities to continue to incorporate the "What, How, Why: Then Justify" approach as discussed in Chapter 1. Also, keep in mind that "tried and true" learning tasks, projects, and assignments are excellent options to upload as opportunities for students to earn badges, items, and XP. Chapter 6 also provides additional enrichment ideas that could easily be integrated as part of a Google Sites simulation.

When uploading any reading materials, it is also fun to integrate some secret words or codes to earn extra XP. Not only does this help to assess who is actually reading through the appropriate reading materials, it is also an unexpected way to continue to add to the simulation experience. This might include a simple statement such as: *Thank you soldier for your continued attention to this assigned task! For an extra 100 XP, email General* (insert name of teacher) *the code word* (insert select word). After integrating these types of XP opportunities, it is amazing how closely students begin to read all the included materials!

Embrace this time to be creative. Have fun with brainstorming potential items that students might like to receive (e.g., the ability to eat lunch in the classroom with a friend, permission to listen to music during independent work time, free homework pass). The items do not have to cost any money at all, yet students will be highly motivated by them. Through the Soldiers of A.L.I.V.E. context, it provides an opportunity to create the items and badges through a military theme, continuing to add to the simulation experience as students strive to become Five Star Generals.

Resource 6 Soldiers of A.L.I.V.E. Handbook

Soldiers of A.L.I.V.E.

American Legions Investigating Virtual Explorations

Introduction

The year is 2870, and you are now an active member of A.L.I.V.E. (American Legions Investigating Virtual Explorations). It is your job, your mission, your life's goal to travel back in time to experience the crude and archaic history of the USA. Along the way, you will be faced with daily challenges, times of war, and economic hardships. As you arrive at your bunker, you will assimilate with other soldiers who have chosen to experience the same quest.

To maintain order, your bunker (class) has been divided into three categories: Battalions, platoons, and regiments. Your ultimate goal is to progress as quickly as possible through each level in order to be ready for the wormhole to take you back to your modern life. Although you need to be responsible for yourself, you will also be required to work within your designated military group to achieve mastery of each level. Your top priority is to collect Leadership Badges, but you will also move up in rankings by earning XP and completing each level.

(Continued)

For each unit, you will be put to the test. Work hard, prove your loyalty, and you will be handsomely rewarded. This journey will not be an easy one. You must dedicate yourself to A.L.I.V.E. in order to survive it. More of the story will follow as your missions unfold.

This handbook will be your guide as you begin to learn about A.L.I.V.E.; you will want to know your goals and what is expected of you in the journey ahead.

Bylaws of A.L.I.V.E.

The bylaws of A.L.I.V.E. are here to make sure that your missions run smoothly. Having clear expectations is paramount! Most importantly, remember to put forth your best effort, continue to persist through times of trial, and take ownership of your work.

Bylaw 1: The Soldier's Honor Code

- Respect the process.
- Respect your peers.
- Respect yourself.
- Respect the work.

Bylaw 2: Leader Badges

- To earn an "A" each grading period, you must have earned a Leader Badge within that time frame.
- An earned Leader Badge does NOT guarantee an "A" in the course.
- Do not procrastinate in earning Leader Badges... there are not endless opportunities.

Bylaw 3: Organizational Protocol

- All items must be stored in your Military Portfolio.
- Only items that are currently stored in your Military Portfolio are able to be redeemed for use.

Bylaw 4: Honesty Pledge

- A.L.I.V.E. does not tolerate any cheating or unethical behavior.
- All judgments made by The General are final.

(Continued)

Bylaw 5: Soldier Responsibilities

- Be personally responsible for your own work and behavior.
- Be a proactive problem-solver!
- All missions must be completed before the end of the unit.

Soldiers of A.L.I.V.E.

Game Terms

Avatar: An in-game image for a student. It represents the virtual persona of the student as Soldier of A.L.I.V.E.

Battalion: One of the smaller assigned groups found within a bunker (class). Students will work closely with this collaborative group through small group activities.

Battle Points: These are points that are found on many items. Battle Points help students during battles (e.g., a class review game, challenges). These points do NOT add to a student's academic score, but they may add to the student's overall XP.

Bunker: The entire class period is referred to as a bunker. Within each bunker, there will be other military divisions. For an elementary teacher, there might only be one bunker, but for a secondary teacher, there could be multiple bunkers based on the different class periods being taught.

Craft: The act of constructing something. This could include a writing project or various other creative projects.

Division: One of the smaller assigned groups found within a bunker (class). Students will work closely with this collaborative group through small group activities.

Item: Items are earned and may be used throughout the simulation to help on various tasks or to make a student's life a little bit easier or more enjoyable. Students should use these items wisely.

Leader Badge: Any badge with LB in the corner counts for the required passport to the "A" range for a graded course. Leader Badges signify required coursework and should be developed to meet the desired learning outcomes for a unit of study. For example, in a World War I unit of study, there might be a Leadership Badge for an activity focused on the Treaty of Versailles. Students should be encouraged to see out as many of these as possible, as they carry a high value of XP.

Level of Honor: A level that signifies a student's level of play as based on current XP standings as determined by the classroom teacher. For example, Level 1 might be determined for students with 0–500 XP, Level 2 for students with 501–1000 XP, and Level 3 for students with 1001 XP and above. These levels are predetermined and communicated by the teacher prior to starting the simulation.

Item Case: The location associated with where the student "houses" their earned items. This might include an online folder or a pocket folder with brads within a traditional classroom setting.

Mini Badge: Any badge that is not an LB is a Mini Badge. These are earned for various challenges within the simulation and represent learning experiences that are

(Continued)

worthwhile and meaningful but might not be directly tied to essential learnings from the unit of study. For example, in a World War I unit of study, there might be a Mini Badge for an activity focused on the controversy related to the sinking of the Lusitania. While these are not LB, they do help students continue to delve deeper into their conceptual understanding of a unit and provide a nice source of additional XP

Platoon: One of the smaller assigned groups found within a bunker (class). Students will work closely with this collaborative group through small group activities.

Player/Soldier: Another name for a student.

Quests: These are the center of A.L.I.V.E. soldier training. Quests are optional activities for students to partake in to earn additional XP, items, and the very best Leader Badges. To succeed within the simulation, students must tackle many quests. Quests fall into three categories:

- ♦ **Solo Quest**: Quest that one must do alone.
- ♦ **Pick-up Quest**: Quest that requires a student to work with a group *outside* of their military group (e.g., battalion, division, platoon).
- ♦ **Military Quest**: Quest that is designed for a student's military group (e.g., battalion, division, platoon) and that group only.

XP: Experience Points that are earned by completing various quests throughout the simulation or compiled through earned items. Those who achieve the highest number of XP by the end of the simulation become 5-Star Generals.

Badges
Badges are the heart of A.L.I.V.E.. Items, described on the next page, help you throughout your journey, but badges are the point of the game. Each badge has a given value assigned to it that will be calculated and added to your XP at the end of the year. The top soldiers will become Five Star Generals of A.L.I.V.E.!

Requirements
To earn an "A" in this course, you need an LB each grading period. NOTICE: Having an LB does NOT mean you get an "A," it means you can earn an "A."

Level of Honor
This is what level you are in during your journey. You must keep this badge in the upper right-hand corner of your military folder or designated organization system. This helps to monitor if you are able to use the items that you are trying to use.

(*Continued*)

Leader Badge (LB)

Any badge with an LB in the corner counts as a Leader Badge. Leader Badges are difficult to earn and are needed to excel in the class. Any badge without the LB in the corner counts as a Mini Badge.

Mini Badge

Badges can be earned by one person, one military group, or one bunker. Mini Badges offer additional opportunities to earn XP and the opportunity to progress in the game.

Items

As a member of A.L.I.V.E., you are able to acquire items that will help you along the way. You will store all earned items in your military folder or designated organizational system.

Most items will have a section that gives a brief explanation of how it works. The name of the item holds no significance to game play. It just adds to the theme of the game. You must reach the level on the card to use the item. If no level is on it, then anyone can use it.

BP stands for Battle Points. BP is found on many items and helps you during class challenges.

The rules for items are explained below.

Requirements: In order to use/hold an item that has a level printed on it, you must have earned that level in your military training.

Item Rules

- All items must be in your military folder or designated organization system.
- Items cannot stack. Stacking means to place more than one item on top of another. You are allowed to place two items per pocket with each facing a different direction.
- You are allowed to trade items.
- No refunds are given!
- No replacements for lost items.
- Only items present count. You will not be allowed to use an item if it is not with you or accessible at that time.

Online access to the Soldiers of A.L.I.V.E. Handbook can also be found at: www.routledge.com/9781646322213

Chapter 6

Continued Engagement and Enrichment through Online and Blended Learning

Thus far, this book has discussed the principles of designing for successful online and blended learning with gifted and advanced learners, explored the importance of evaluating online learning resources and tasks, and detailed how some popular online applications can be used to create engaging and challenging learning opportunities for this population. With the continued evolution of instructional technology, there is simply no way to provide a context for every available online learning resource; however, the goal of this book is to empower and enlighten continued innovative thinking. As such, this chapter focuses on additional avenues to explore when continuing to grow through technology-focused instructional methods.

As you continue to stretch yourself by implementing new ideas and searching for new approaches to engage and challenge gifted and advanced learners, it is often helpful to reflect upon the types of in-person activities that your students enjoy participating in within the traditional classroom setting and begin to brainstorm ideas that come to mind. These might include anything from hands-on learning activities such as labs or constructions, field trips, or quite simply just being provided with choice of activity.

Once you have your list, reflect on "how" that approach, method, or context continues to meet the unique learning needs of gifted and advanced learners. For example, providing choice is wonderful, but if the choices do not include the level of depth and complexity needed to provide challenging and engaging learning experiences, then it is a missed opportunity. Similarly, field trip experiences should always include an opportunity for continued inquiry, connection to abstract conceptual understanding, and reflective synthesis of the experience, itself. While this is a bit more of a challenge through the use of technology, it is absolutely possible. This chapter continues to discuss how to bring continued engagement and enrichment to online learning through a variety of instructional approaches.

Virtual Field Trips

In a typical year, most students look forward to and have wonderful memories of their field trip experiences. Whether they are able to visit a specific museum, view the celestial sky at a

DOI: 10.4324/9781003238317-6

planetarium, or take a nature hike at a forest preserve, students are immersed in learning through these experiences. While it is not *exactly* the same, technology does provide us with field trip opportunities that many of our students might never be able to experience due to geographical restrictions, financial concerns, or other circumstances. Through the online context, virtual field trips open the door to even greater opportunities for learning, whether students are able to walk along the Great Wall of China or visit the Louvre.

In much the same way that students engage with video game technology, virtual field trips allow students to navigate through desired destinations, exploring through a 360° view of their surroundings. Teaching through this type of virtual reality maintains advanced learning that leads to discovery (Donally, 2019) and provides gifted and advanced learners with a fully immersive experience (Huang et al., 2019).

In today's ever-changing world of technology, do not hesitate in conducting a few online searches of your own to find opportunities for new sites, links, and available destinations, but in the meantime, Table 6.1 provides an overview of some popular destinations to include as part of an individual or group field-trip experience. Consider embedding virtual field trips within online simulations (see Chapters 4 and 5), escape rooms (see Chapter 4), Bitmoji classrooms, or choice boards (see end of chapter) as you continue to look for ways to engage gifted and advanced learners in the academic process.

The Purpose behind the Plan

As previously mentioned, all field trips should allow students the opportunity for engaged inquiry and continued conceptual understanding through reflection and synthesis of learning. With this in mind, be purposeful in the selection of virtual field trip experiences. Consider the following guiding questions when seeking to integrate virtual field trips into your instruction:

♦ Which standards are addressed through the integration of the virtual field trip experience?
♦ How does the virtual field trip support the desired learning objective(s)?
♦ How will the learning objective(s) be assessed?
♦ What types of learning activities align with the virtual field trip?
♦ How might one or more universal themes and generalizations (e.g., power, chaos vs. order, exploration, change) be integrated into the virtual field trip experience?
♦ How might the virtual field trip integrate cross-curricular opportunities for learning?

As these questions are addressed, there will be greater purpose behind the plan, opening the door to greater depth of learning.

There are also many supplemental activities that can stem from and contribute to virtual field trips. When designing these online learning experiences, remain mindful of providing gifted and advanced learners with the opportunity to engage in deeper levels of critical thinking. While there are many options, the following are activities that work well across a variety of virtual field trip experiences:

Metaphorical Mind-Maps

♦ Generalization Journals
♦ I Spy (and This is Why)

Table 6.1 Popular Virtual Field-Trip Destinations: A Sampling of Sites

Site Destinations and Links
Travel around the world with Google Arts and Culture. (Make sure to search for the "Explore" image within each destination to experience a 360° visual experience through the various options.) https://artsandculture.google.com/partner?hl=en
The Great Wall of China. https://www.thechinaguide.com/destination/great-wall-of-china
The Louvre https://www.louvre.fr/en/visites-en-ligne#tabs
Smithsonian National Museum of Natural History https://naturalhistory.si.edu/visit/virtual-tour
A wide selection of destinations, including underwater experiences https://www.360cities.net
The National Aquarium https://aqua.org/media/virtualtours/baltimore/index.html
Virtual Planetarium https://stellarium-web.org/
Colonial Williamsburg https://www.colonialwilliamsburg.org/learn/virtual-tours/

- ◆ Perspective Dive
- ◆ Scavenger Hunt

Metaphorical Mind-Maps

A metaphorical mind-map is an instructional tool to help students connect seemingly "unlike" materials and make cross-curricular connections. For example, perhaps students are learning about paleontology in earth science, but in social studies they are learning about the Civil War. In an effort to help students delve deeper into their conceptual understanding of both, a virtual field trip to the Smithsonian National Museum of Natural History (found at https://naturalhistory.si.edu/visit/virtual-tour) might be a useful field trip.

While virtually exploring the museum and making connections to what they are learning in earth science, students would also be tasked with creating metaphorical mind-maps of how the two seemingly separate units of study share metaphorical commonalities. For instance, perhaps the battle tactics from a historic battle might be metaphorically compared to the strategic hunting practices of velociraptors.

The format of metaphorical mind-maps could also take the form of a typical concept-map (see Chapter 4), where students brainstorm and write key terms, connecting "like" terms together with lines as they continue to build out further connections and details. This could be completed through a variety of online applications that are free and easily integrated into online learning, or students could complete a concept-map on paper to be turned in either in-person or by submitting a scan or picture of the completed activity. Often, it is helpful to have a structured template to guide students in their metaphorical thinking, so Resource 7 provides a graphic organizer to help students as they engage in their thinking throughout the virtual field trip experience.

Resource 7 Metaphorical Mind-Map Organizer

Directions: After writing the overarching content areas in the spaces at the top of the page, use the boxes in the two end columns to specify each content-specific item, event, or concept. In the center column describe the comparison of how the two corresponding content-specific examples are metaphorically similar.

Content Area#1 _____ ↓ Content-Specific Example ↓	Metaphorical Comparison How are the two content-specific examples alike? Make sure you describe specific details to signify their metaphorical connection. ↓	Content Area #2 _____ ↓ Content-Specific Example ↓

As an alternate approach, students could create a visual metaphor, using images and art to represent the metaphorical connections that were made between the two seemingly separate subject areas. In using the Civil War and velociraptor example above, the visual metaphor could illustrate how these two seemingly separate entities have commonalities by having velociraptors in uniform at a specific battle that illustrates the similar "battle" tactics.

Regardless of whatever form the metaphorical mind-map takes, each of these options can be completed through a variety of online applications that are free and easily integrated into a variety of learning management systems.

Generalization Journal

Virtual field trips are yet another opportunity to engage gifted and advanced learners with making connections to universal themes and generalizations (see Chapter 1). This is easily done by having students keep a Generalization Journal of their personal experiences with the virtual field trip. Whether the students use an online journal/document, or you create a Google Form with guided journal entries, this activity continues to help students engage with the virtual field trip experience.

Within the journal, students write about what they are seeing, experiencing, and learning throughout the field trip. This might include descriptive accounts of what is visually represented at the specific destination, as well as their experiences in navigating through the destination. As students write about what they are learning and experiencing as part of the virtual field trip, they are also tasked with connecting the different exhibits, observations, and/or experiences to a selected universal theme and its accompanying generalizations. Depending on the desired outcomes, students might be assigned a universal theme, or it might be open to choice. For example, if students are taking a virtual field trip to the Great Wall of China, they could be tasked with making connections to the universal theme of chaos vs. order. In doing so, they would include within their journal entries, connections of their field trip experience and related content to the associated generalizations of:

- ♦ Order leads to chaos and chaos leads to order
- ♦ Order may be natural or constructed
- ♦ Order may allow for prediction
- ♦ Order is a form of communication
- ♦ Order may have repeated patterns
- ♦ Order and chaos are reciprocals

Of course, other universal themes such as power, change, conflict, etc. could be used, as well. When working with Generalization Journals, it is helpful to provide specific guidelines regarding the number of required entries. As a means to encourage a greater number of journal entries, it is recommended to use the *at least* parameters (i.e., at least eight journal entries).

I Spy (and This Is Why)

Similar to the Generalization Journal, this strategy directs students to explore the virtual field trip through comparing, contrasting, and analyzing the various implications of the field trip destination, itself. In this activity, the purpose of the virtual field trip is to have students make observations in their learning and compare those insights to the modern world in which they live. For instance, if the virtual field trip is to an art museum, the students would target specific works of art and compare the images to current times, examining the subject of the art, the theme of the art, and the historical context behind the art. Each of these would be compared and contrasted with the current times. Students would then make connections to the possible implications from when the selection was created, as well as the implications for the art's theme in today's current times.

Perspective Dive

This purposeful activity continues to provide gifted and advanced learners with exploring a virtual field trip through a different perspective. For instance, imagine if you were experiencing a virtual field trip to Colonial Williamsburg through the lens of a British Redcoat, a Patriot, a Loyalist, a slave, or an indigenous person from that time period. Each of these perspectives would notice different aspects to this experience and be treated in different ways.

Through the Perspective Dive strategy, students place themselves "within" the time period as a means to broaden and expand their insights into how the historical time period, culture, and accepted mindsets impacted different populations of people. Again, this strategy can be completed through an online journal/document or through the use of guiding questions through a Google Form.

Scavenger Hunt

Through the Virtual Scavenger Hunt, students are provided a list of items, sightings, or destinations to locate throughout their virtual field trip experience. By providing a list to students, the objectives of the virtual field trip are often easier to ascertain, as students are better directed to locate, study, and respond to questions focused on specific items of interest. Not only does this help students engage with and explore the entire virtual field trip location, it also provides students with clear expectations of what they are searching for and what they need to accomplish before the virtual field trip is completed. Consider providing students with direct questions that will help them engage with the required artifacts and/or virtual experiences.

Putting It All Together

All in all, virtual field trips provide an avenue to keep students engaged through online learning by providing an immersive experience. While the aforementioned strategies are just a sampling of ideas, it is also possible to combine them to create more complex learning activities as you continue to differentiate for online instruction. For instance, consider having students participate in a virtual field trip scavenger hunt that also includes a perspective dive, or students could create a metaphorical mind-map in conjunction with a generalization journal. Regardless of which instructional strategies are selected, the main goal is to provide gifted and advanced learners with purposeful interaction throughout the virtual field trip experience.

Choice Boards

Choice Boards, often referred to as Show What You Know Boards, provide an opportunity to differentiate learning based on content, process, and product. Set up very similar to a tic-tac-toe board or learning menu, an online choice board provides students with a variety of tasks, complete with links and directions. Students are then directed to complete one or more of the various options. Students are allowed to work in a random manner, choosing a specific number of tasks to complete, or in a more structured manner by completing one activity from each row and connecting their selections (e.g., three-in-a-row, 2×2 postage stamp), or complete tasks based off of other specified directives (e.g., select one from each color-code). Choice boards can be created for projects, weekly tasks, homework, and/or assessments and provide students with the ability to choose *how* they would like to demonstrate their personalized levels of learning. By providing student choice in this manner, higher levels of motivation and engagement in the learning process ensue.

While designing choice boards for use with online and blended learning, the first consideration is deciding if the choice board will be focused on teaching a specific area of content (e.g., the middle ages, plate tectonics, a specific genre of reading/writing) or a specific skill (e.g., solving for unknown variables, main idea, identifying independent and dependent variables, figurative language). The next step involves brainstorming ideas that include a variety of your students' interests and value systems (see Chapter 2), as well as a variety of formats to demonstrate levels of understanding (e.g., writing, artistic representation, computation, construction). While it is often common for teachers to include a *free space*, it is strongly recommended to adapt that space into a space for students to create and complete an activity of their own development, which would be dependent on teacher approval.

When working with gifted and advanced learners, in particular, all choice board components should offer challenging activities to guide them deeper into their critical thinking and problem-solving. As such, be mindful to provide a variety of activities that continue to support the Integrated Curriculum Model (VanTassel-Baska, 2009) through advanced content, advanced processes, and connection to advanced concepts.

Unfortunately, many readily available and accessible online choice boards do not provide the level of challenge to better meet these needs, leading to disengagement and underachievement of gifted and advanced learners. Refer to Table 1.2 as you evaluate these pre-made online resources for your classroom. If designing original online choice boards, Table 6.2 provides suggestions for various components that could be adapted and developed for any unit of study. Suggestions for how to adapt online choice board options for students without access to technology at home are also provided.

Regardless of which activities are included as part of the choice board, ensure that clear directions, expectations for completion, and any required links to complete the various tasks are included. Additional ideas might include activities that include SCAMPER or creating an infographic, podcast, game, comic strip, pic collage, or timeline/diagram.

Table 6.2 Choice Board Activity Options for Gifted and Advanced Learners

Choice Board Activity	Description	Non-technology Adaptation
Museum Exhibit	Students create an online museum exhibit focused on the desired content (e.g., author study, battles of the Civil War, polygons, specific vocabulary). The exhibit could be created through the design of a website, an online document with links, or as part of a presentation (e.g., Google Slides, PowerPoint, Prezi). Each artifact included in the "museum" should provide a hyperlink or QR code to a visual representation, description of impact to the content area, and connection to a universal theme and generalizations.	Provide print materials and resources to help a student complete the needed research for the museum exhibit. Students may draw or construct models of their displayed artifacts. All necessary written components may be completed by hand.
Double Fishbone (Mofield & Phelps, 2020)	Have students complete a Double Fishbone (See Chapter 4) to demonstrate their understanding of the causes and effects of a chosen topic (e.g., graph data, event in a story, scientific problem, historical event). An online Double Fishbone is easily completed on Jamboard (see end of chapter) or similar online learning tool. Make sure to provide students with online access to the focused content.	Provide students with a hardcopy of the Double Fishbone template, as well as hardcopies of the content being used to complete the Double Fishbone.
Double Acrostic	The double acrostic provides students with a specific word, and students are directed to write a sentence that begins AND ends with each letter in the chosen word. For example, if the students are given the word "ENERGY" while	Provide students with a hardcopy of the double acrostic chosen word template which includes the letters of the chosen word on each side of the page with connecting lines to write the created sentences or phrases.

(Continued)

Table 6.2 (Continued)

Choice Board Activity	Description	Non-technology Adaptation
	learning about sustainable fuels, a student might write the first line as *Every fuel source should be environmentally friendly and safe for the global climatE.* The remaining lines of the double acrostic for this guiding word would begin and end with the remaining letters of N, E, R, G, and Y. (see additional example in Table 2.1). This can be completed through any online document or application of choice (e.g., Google Doc, Padlet).	
100 Words or Less	Students are directed to write an analysis connected to the chosen topic of study in 100 words or less. This can be completed through any online document or application of choice (e.g., Google Doc, Padlet).	Students are able to complete a handwritten response to be turned in.
Alpha Boxes	Students are tasked with finding a word, image, object, or representation tied to a topic of study that represents each letter of the alphabet. For example, when studying a unit on The Progressive Era, a student might include Carnegie for the letter C, Muckrakers for the letter M, and the Triangle Shirtwaist Factory for the letter T. Along with each letter's representation, students should also provide a short description and/or background about the chosen word, image, or object.	Provide an Alpha Box template that provides a designated box or space for each letter of the alphabet. Students will be able to complete this template in lieu of an online completion.

Virtual Showcase

Whether students have completed independent study projects, constructed individualized works of art, conducted science fair experiments, or developed solutions to address real-world problems, the conundrum arises on how students can present their learning experiences through an online distance model. Virtual Showcase provides a solution to this problem.

Through a virtual showcase, students are provided with an opportunity to create an online presentation to share their work. Once students submit their presentations, they are compiled into one venue to be shared with the identified audience. This might be with the class, itself, or could expand to include families, communities, or even experts in a particular field of study. While one option is for students to present "live" as part of a Zoom or TEAMS session, virtual showcases open the possibility of creating a showcase of saved work that could be accessed within any given time frame or availability window.

As with any access to student work, it is a top priority to remain cognizant of student confidentiality. In knowing what access your students and families have to technology, be mindful of including passwords, sharing links to content only with the desired audience, and even collecting permission slips from families if the virtual showcase is going to be accessible to others outside of your classroom community. Another key factor to consider is not posting students' full names, ages, geographical location, or other identifying information. The great news is that virtual showcases are highly successful without including any of this identifiable information.

Interestingly enough, while many students freeze at the idea of presenting their information in person, the idea of sharing their learning through a virtual showcase is exciting and liberating, as it allows the opportunity to pre-record the various components while also providing a context to be creative in how they decide to share their work. As you plan for the virtual showcase, it is important to set clear expectations from the onset of the activity. All students, not just gifted and advanced learners, work better when there is structure in place, and they know what needs to be accomplished. The requirements for a virtual showcase are no different. The following sections will discuss these requirements in more detail.

Virtual Showcase: Easy as P.I.E.

While a virtual showcase can be adapted, reframed, and modified, at its basic stance, it consists of three guiding components: Presentation, Info-graphic, and what is commonly referred to as an Elevator pitch. When these three components come together, it is represented through the acronym of PIE. Within each of the individual components there are ample opportunities for continued differentiation, as well as endless possibilities for creativity and self-expression. As such, it is important to remind students to keep their submissions professional and school appropriate.

Depending on the content area or purpose for the virtual showcase, Table 6.3 provides the Example Rubric With Differentiation Features (Mofield & Phelps, 2020), which is easily

Table 6.3 Example Rubric with Differentiation Features

	4-Exceeds Expectations	3-Meets Expectations	2-Approaches Expectations and Needs Effort	1-Needs Effort
Content	Demonstrates application of advanced vocabulary, language of the discipline, and accurate portrayal of newly learned content. Makes insightful connections to other content within and outside the discipline. Student supplies additional criteria: _____	Demonstrates application of grade-level vocabulary, language of the discipline, and accurate portrayal of newly learned content. Makes some connections to content within and outside the discipline.	Demonstrates some application of grade-level vocabulary, language of the discipline, and portrayal of newly learned content, though some elements may be missing. Only loose connections are made to content within or outside the discipline.	Does not demonstrate adequate application of grade-level vocabulary, language of the discipline, and portrayal of newly learned content. Little or no connections are made to content within or outside the discipline.
Creative Thinking	Shows substantive evidence of many, varied, elaborate, and/or original ideas applied to the content.	Shows some evidence of many, varied, elaborate, and/or original ideas applied to content.	Shows little evidence of fluent, varied, elaborate, and/or original thinking applied to content.	Does not show evidence of creative thinking. Demonstrates only summary of facts.
Critical Thinking	Demonstrates logical reasoning through perspective taking, use of evidence, and implications of thinking. Applies the	Demonstrates some logical reasoning through perspective taking, use of evidence, and implications of thinking. Applies the	Demonstrates some reasoning, though there might be gaps in connections and logical explanations. Use of perspective taking, evidence,	Little or no evidence of logical reasoning throughout the product.

(Continued)

Table 6.3 (Continued)

	4-Exceeds Expectations	3-Meets Expectations	2-Approaches Expectations and Needs Effort	1-Needs Effort
	thinking process of an expert in the field (thinking as a historian, etc.).	thinking process of an expert in the field (thinking as a historian, etc.).	and implications can be improved.	
Product	High-quality product is reflective of what an expert might produce in the field or discipline.	High-quality product demonstrates learning related to the content area.	Product demonstrates learning related to the content area.	Product lacks detail and/or does not adequately reflect content learning.

Source: From Collaboration, Coteaching, and Coaching in Gifted Education: Sharing Strategies to Support Gifted Learners, by E. Mofield and V. Phelps, 2020, Prufrock Press. Reprinted with permission of the authors.

adapted to a variety of topics and subject areas to help guide and focus gifted and advanced learners in the development of the virtual showcase. In addition, Roberts and Inman's (2015) Developing and Assessing Product (DAP) Tools are also helpful in developing and assessing student learning in this context, as ceilings are lifted and students are stretched to think as professionals and disciplinarians in a specific field of study.

Presentation

Regardless of the content or focus of the virtual showcase, students will need to create a presentation to showcase their work. Popular options include slide decks from PowerPoint presentations, Google Slides presentations, and Prezi's, but encourage students to think outside the box and explore other options. This is a wonderful opportunity for students to grow and evolve within the ever-changing technological world.

At the core of this component, students will need to provide an overview of the key components of their project through written and visual means. While the presentation could include a recorded oral presentation, the elevator pitch will also include a verbal introduction to the subject-matter. Students need to prioritize what information is key to understanding the presentation, itself. Helpful guiding questions include:

♦ How will you gain the audience's attention? What is the hook?
♦ What is the purpose of this presentation?
♦ What steps did you go through during this project?
♦ What assumptions might need to be addressed with regard to this subject-matter?
♦ What are the key takeaways the viewer should learn from this presentation?

Infographic

The infographic is a standalone representation of the key takeaways of the subject-matter of the presentation (see example at https://tinyurl.com/y5s4m97x). This could be a brochure or single page infographic. Students should be provided with an example to guide their thinking, and while the key components will be different based on different areas of focus, a guiding model will help the gifted and advanced learners apply their own subject-matter to this task. Key questions to help guide students in the development of their infographics include:

♦ What type of statistical information should be included to support your topic?
♦ Given that there is a great deal of interesting facts on your topic, how might you use the strategy of determining importance to select the main components for your infographic?
♦ How might you incorporate visual representations of your subject-focus?
♦ How might you integrate a variety of fonts, sizes, and colors of texts to add visual aesthetic to your infographic?

Elevator Pitch

The elevator pitch is a short video, 1–3 minutes in length, where the student(s) provide a spoken overview of their content. As signified by the name, students have to imagine that they only have the time allotted by a typical elevator ride to convince someone their idea is worth pursuing further and learning more about. While most students feel comfortable with being the subject of these short videos, remain mindful that some students might feel very uncomfortable with seeing themselves on camera. In these cases, allow the student(s) to explore other approaches (e.g., Powtoon, bitmoji,voiceover with appropriate images) to the elevator pitch. In essence, the purpose and objective of the elevator pitch should not be on the actual "face" of the presenter, but rather on the communication of key content. As previously mentioned, remain mindful of student confidentiality by not sharing names, ages, geographic locations, etc. as part of any publicly shared presentations. It is strongly suggested to share the virtual showcase with only an identified audience through password protection or direct link access.

An Example of Practice

Online learning offers a successful avenue for independent study. Whether students are learning research skills through distance learning, a class is participating in online Genius Hour, or a single student has demonstrated content mastery and needs curriculum compacting, independent study serves as an easily managed online differentiation strategy to help gifted and advanced learners pursue an area of interest while being stretched in their own thinking. As previously discussed through virtual field trips, online independent study needs to be purposeful. While students should be given choice in the topic of research, there should be clear expectations for the process itself, as well as ongoing feedback and interaction with the teacher. Table 6.4 provides an overview of the I-LEARN Process (Phelps, 2021) as adapted to online learning. This structure continues to support gifted and advanced learners through independent study while providing clear expectations and guidelines for each step of the research process.

When using the I-LEARN Process in conjunction with a virtual showcase, the presentation, infographic, and elevator pitch would all be integrated within the required

Table 6.4 I-LEARN Steps Adapted to Creating Successful Online Independent Study

	I-LEARN Steps	**To-Do List for Online Independent Study**
I	Identify a Topic to Investigate	1. Determine if the online independent study should focus on a deeper, more complex examination of pre-assessment content (e.g., thinking as a disciplinarian to solve a related world issue with applied skills), or should the independent study be based on student interest? 2. Include the student in the I-LEARN Process. 3. Decide if the independent study will be approached through description, cause/effect, comparison, or problem/solution. 4. Determine the form of research the independent study will take (e.g., case study, explanatory, historical, correlation, experimental, action).
L	Lay out a Learning Plan	1. Create an Online Independent Learning Contract to be signed, or agreed upon, by the student, teacher, and parent. 2. Create a list of learning components (e.g., presentation, infographic, elevator pitch) with accompanying rubrics. When selecting these tasks, provide the student with options, and outline what is expected for successful completion of each task. 3. Establish what materials (e.g., notebook, graphic organizers, reflection sheets, sources, handouts) are needed for this independent study and how they will be stored and accessed online. 4. Determine what types of resources will be utilized to accomplish the I-LEARN goals. (e.g., books, videos, interviews, computer programs, online applications/tools) 5. Construct a timeline for completion dates along with pre-established check-in dates.
E	Engage in Research	1. Create guiding research question(s). 2. Establish how the research will be organized and maintained through an online learning management system (e.g., Google Classroom, Canvas, Blackboard). 3. Determine how sources will be cited.
A	Apply Learning	1. Create an authentic culminating task for synthesis of learned information with an accompanying rubric (e.g., virtual showcase) 2. Identify real-world connection/application.

(Continued)

Table 6.4 (Continued)

	I-LEARN Steps	To-Do List for Online Independent Study
R	Reflect and Refine	1. Determine how student reflection will be part of the independent study process. 2. Create specific questions to guide the student in the reflective/refinement process of learning. (e.g., *What did I do well? What would I do differently?*) 3. Specify how the teacher will provide additional feedback during the scheduled check-ins through an online meeting space, as well as through consistent feedback through the selected learning management system.
N	Next Steps for Newfound Knowledge	1. Determine how the components of learning will be shared with an identified audience. 2. Identify potential next steps for future research.

Note: Adapted from "Differentiation Through Independent Study: The I-LEARN Process," by V. Phelps, in A. Quinzio-Zafran and E. Wilkins (Eds.), *The New Teacher's Guide to Overcoming Common Challenges: Curated Advice From Award Winning Teachers*, 2021, Routledge.

components of the I-LEARN Process, and once students have completed their independent study, they will share their learning through the Virtual Showcase.

A Few More Helpful Sites

As previously stated, technology is a constantly evolving field, so it is near impossible to include cutting-edge applications and sites when publishing a print resource. To stay abreast of the newest trends and approaches to technology education, consider joining different groups through social media or through websites. It is extremely helpful to learn from innovators in the field about new tools and approaches to online and blended learning. The following are a small sampling of additional references and tools found to be helpful in online and blended learning:

♦ **The Padagogy Wheel** (Reddin et al., 2017): This instructional tool provides a guide which ultimately connects a plethora of online applications and learning tools with Bloom's (1956) taxonomy. In doing so, this resource (found at http://bit.ly/PWENGV5) aligns the levels of thinking (i.e., remember, understand, apply, analyze, evaluate, create) with action words, activities, and online applications to further enhance student learning within each of these cognitive levels.

The Padagogy Wheel also serves as a well-researched differentiation tool for gifted and advanced learners. It can be utilized from the onset of instructional design to help inform and guide the development of online learning to encompass the top tiers of Bloom's taxonomy (i.e., analyze, evaluate, create). It can also be used to differentiate student assignments based on levels of readiness. Whether it is used as a means to help create online choice boards or provide students with ideas to implement within their independent study, it is a helpful visual to easily reference within any traditional classroom or Bitmoji classroom.

♦ **Flippity.net:** As you have probably noticed within the context of this book, several references have been made to flippity.net. While this website hosts a variety of online instructional tools that can be implemented and further modified to better meet the needs of gifted and advanced learners. Of the many tools available on this site, there are three that have been very useful in working with gifted and advanced learners.

- **Flippity Manipulatives:** Using inductive reasoning (Taba et al., 1971), students virtually sort key vocabulary/items/phrases/equations/etc., develop categories, and create generalizations about a topic of study.

- **Flippity Scavenger Hunt:** Create a series of locks and keys to engage students through solving equations, searching for key content, or problem-solving riddles and advanced content.

- **Flippity Randomizer:** Challenge gifted and advanced learners to refine guiding research questions, write through different perspectives, or examine complex topics. The Randomizer Wheel can be used through a variety of applications.

♦ **Jamboard:** Resembling a collaborative whiteboard for students, Jamboard provides a collaborative workspace for students to plan, process, and design content. As part of Google Drive, it is also very easily integrated into a variety of Google applications. The teacher may provide basic information on a Jamboard as a means to guide student learning, or students may use this space to create solutions to identified problems, develop presentations to share research, or respond to advanced questions and ponderings. Jamboard allows for limitless possibilities in collaborative work.

Regardless of which tools you choose to integrate into your online instruction, be creative and look "beyond" the surface level of how that particular application can be used. Whether you are creating a Jeopardy style review game or a matching game, continue to be mindful of creating opportunities for gifted and advanced learners to think deeply about advanced content and make connections to abstract concepts.

Chapter 7

Supporting Parents and Guardians as Collaborative Partners in Online Learning

The chapters in this book have explored a small sampling of how instructional design through technology can best support gifted and advanced learners through online and blended learning experiences. Various options have been shared through integrating technology within the traditional classroom as a differentiation tool, as part of blended learning offering consistent enrichment, or through dedicated, ongoing distance learning. With each of these scenarios, there are varying levels and degrees of parental/guardian support that are needed.

More often than naught, parents/guardians are busy juggling the demands of work, multiple children, lack of technology access, and/or running a household, while still trying to maintain a life balance for their family. In working to support their children who are engaged in online instruction, it is also necessary to communicate clearly and consistently, seek their insights, and provide suggestions on how they can best support their child's learning. When designing online and blended learning experiences for gifted and advanced students, remain cognizant that parental/guardian support and involvement is pivotal in student success (Robinson et al., 2007).

Keeping Parents and Guardians in the Conversation

At the very least, frequent communication with parents and guardians is foundational to successful online and blended learning. With current learning management systems (e.g., SeeSaw, Canvas, Blackboard, Google Classroom), parents and guardians have the opportunity to access and monitor their child's assignments, due dates, and grades, but even with this knowledge, they are often unsure how to help support their children within the online learning process, itself. In part, this is due to the fact that many do not understand how to

DOI: 10.4324/9781003238317-7

truly navigate these various learning management systems, let alone know how to support the more advanced learning tasks that are assigned to gifted and advanced learners.

In an effort to monitor the level and type of communication with parents and guardians, it is a good idea to keep a communication log to keep track of consistent and meaningful communication that is focused on supporting online learning at home. This can be kept through an online document of your choosing (e.g., word document, spreadsheet) or even in an old-fashioned notebook. Regardless of how the information is collected and stored, it serves as a means to be mindful and accountable in recognizing that parents/guardians are productive partners in education.

It is also important to consider the types of communication that are utilized. While a great deal of information can be sent out via email, notification apps, and updated web pages, it is necessary to create opportunities for two-way communication as a means to improve at-home support and enhance the online learning experience (Martin, 2020). Within all communications, it is also paramount to incorporate inclusive and welcoming language that continues to build collaborative relationships (Mofield & Phelps, 2020). This includes being aware and respectful of families' cultures, family structures, and primary languages (Allen, 2007). It is also equally important to communicate with purpose and without educational jargon or acronyms (e.g., RTI, ICM, KWL, Venn, formative assessment) without explanation (Martin, 2020). Terms that are part of the day-to-day vocabulary for educators are often a foreign language to those outside of the field.

Recognizing the Struggle

As educators, it is easy to fall into the mindset that we are putting forth a great deal of effort in our planning, and in doing so, we feel comfortably certain that students, especially gifted and advanced learners and families, will be able to know *exactly* what is expected through online and blended learning while away from the traditional classroom. Through blended learning scenarios, teachers have a much better opportunity to communicate with students in person during traditional classroom instruction. However, during exclusive online instruction, especially due to mandated, distance learning in response to a pandemic, natural disaster, or other unforeseen circumstance, the role of parents and guardians as "at-home educational partners" has the potential to create additional stressors and challenges to the online learning environment. For example, during the COVID-19 pandemic, parents/guardians expressed the following reasons for struggles with online, distance learning (Houston Independent School District, 2020):

◆ There were too many independent assignments to complete (i.e., quantity over quality)
◆ The work was not challenging enough
◆ Communication from schools and teachers was unclear
◆ Technical difficulties/Lack of understanding
◆ Lack of student accountability
◆ Lack of differentiation

In knowing these concerns, a greater understanding of how to prioritize communications is clarified. Whether it is something as simple as helping parents/guardians recognize how to help their child navigate uploading documents to submit or raising awareness about the loopholes of how students might seem to "submit" work in order to remove the task from the visible required work list (without the student actually submitting the work), there are helpful tips to communicate how to successfully navigate and support online learning as well as the expectations of assigned work.

In addition, it is often common to think that gifted and advanced learners need *more* tasks because of their ability. This is a fallacy. Gifted and advanced learners need *different* tasks and instructional approaches because of their unique learning needs. Take the time to create quality, online instruction versus creating quantity or focusing on using every new technology application that is made available (EEF, 2020). Often, the depth and complexity in learning is lost when this focus is lost. Also, remain mindful that real-time learning activities have been found to increase student engagement (Lucas et al., 2020). Taking the extra time to schedule additional online meeting times will be well worth it!

Proactive Planning

As you plan for meaningful communication with parents and guardians, recognize what potential challenges could lie ahead for your population of students (e.g., lack of access to the internet, multiple family members sharing one computer, multilingual families). Be proactive and plan to address these challenges in your ongoing communications. Set a goal to integrate mini-lessons into instruction to model and better prepare students on how to navigate new applications to learning, and provide parents/guardians with guidance on how to problem-solve and navigate the nuances of online learning. Ask yourself, "How might these challenges be integrated into my online instructional practice to enhance the learning process, hold students accountable, and maintain high levels of motivation and engagement?"

The first step in addressing these issues is taking the time to recognize and truly listen to the shared concerns of parents and guardians in regard to supporting online learning at home. McGuinness (2020) found that most of these concerns focused on:

♦ Uncertainty in how to support content-specific knowledge
♦ Difficulty in motivating the child to complete online learning at home
♦ The lack of socialization associated with online learning
♦ The need for more directive, online meeting space instruction
♦ The struggle of balancing parental work demands while also supporting online learning for children

Once these various concerns are acknowledged, then possible solutions can be developed to better support the online learning needs of gifted and advanced learners. Table 7.1 provides suggestions for how to address these different areas of concern. By addressing many of the identified areas of needed support, the stress placed on parents and guardians as "at home teaching assistants" is subsequently diminished.

Table 7.1 Suggestions for Supporting Parents and Guardians as Partners through Online Learning

Area of Needed Support (McGuinness, 2020)	Suggestions for Support

Increase Content-Area Knowledge	◆ Include links to reference materials (e.g., articles, videos, charts, labeled diagrams) for parents and guardians to support understanding of content.
	◆ Provide sample responses for similar assignments (e.g., sample problems with solutions provided, structure/guidelines of what should be included in a response).
	◆ Provide question-stems to parents/guardians to engage in deeper conversations with their child about related topics. For example,
	  • How can you relate what you learned about ____ to something in your own life?
	  • In what ways might we be able to use what you learned about _____ to help us at home?
	  • Given what you learned about _____, how might you create a metaphor or analogy for that topic?

Increase Motivation	◆ Be clear on the purpose for each assignment. ◆ Incorporate students' task valuation (see Chapter 2). ◆ Provide a structure for at-home online learning. ◆ Incorporate virtual field trips, scavenger hunts, choice boards, etc. (see Chapter 6). ◆ Incorporate gamification (e.g., badges, XP) into online learning tasks as a means to increase sustained motivation (see Chapter 5).
Improve Socialization	◆ Integrate interactions for students to have greater opportunities for online discussions and partner activities through breakout rooms. ◆ Consider how to implement more collaborative learning opportunities into online instruction (see Chapter 2).

(Continued)

Table 7.1 (Continued)

Area of Needed Support (McGuinness, 2020)	Suggestions for Support
	♦ Consider hosting an afterschool online extracurricular club (e.g., book club, math club, cooking club, gaming club). ♦ Seek out additional community opportunities to engage with others (e.g., university sponsored gifted/enrichment courses, local gifted associations, MENSA meetings).
Time with Direct Instruction	♦ Be mindful that ample, direct instruction is provided through online meeting spaces and not just videos, assignments, and self-taught opportunities for learning. ♦ Incorporate a flipped-classroom instructional approach to encourage online meeting times to be more focused on discussions and deeper examination of advanced content. ♦ Provide clearly communicated office-hours for students in need of additional instruction. This can be easily accomplished through an online meeting space.

Structures for Success

Whether online learning is part of ongoing distance learning or gifted and advanced students are completing online learning tasks at home as part of blended and/or enrichment learning, having a clear "at-home" structure creates greater opportunities for success. Table 7.2 provides an overview of helpful structures that lead to successful online learning. When communicating and collaborating with parents and guardians, consider using these ideas as topics for newsletters, updates, or blog posts as a means to raise awareness of research in the field.

Table 7.2 At-Home Structures for Successful Online Learning

Focused Area	At-Home Recommendations
Learning Space	◆ When possible, have a dedicated learning space away from distractions (e.g., television, video games, high traffic area in the home). ◆ Allow the child to personalize the learning space if possible (e.g., personal artwork, statements of affirmation, comfortable seating).
Time Management	◆ Provide a designated time each day for online learning. ◆ Allow for breaks (e.g., movement break, snack break, "recess"). ◆ Utilize a calendar (e.g., wall, pocket, online) to designate due dates, chart progress, and prioritize learning task completion.
Work Completion	◆ Be mindful when providing reinforcements to easily accessed items (e.g., iPads, video games, candy) as a reward for work completion, as they diminish the effectiveness of the incentive (McGuinnes, 2020). ◆ Create incentives that are considered valuable, such as one-on-one time with a parent (e.g., go on a nature hike, play a board game, bake a cake) or other more cherished activities. ◆ Continue to provide breaks. ◆ Celebrate the effort in completing the task rather than the final product. ◆ Break longer assignments into more manageable tasks. For example, when working on a virtual showcase (see Chapter 6), break the whole task into different components(e.g., develop a guiding research question, research, infographic, elevator pitch, presentation). Set goals for when each task will be completed.

Compliance	◆ Be mindful in monitoring the child's behavior before, during, and after online learning (McGuinnes, 2020).
	  • Spend time providing attention *before* the student engages in online learning to address emotional and psychosocial needs, leading to a decrease in craved attention and acting out *during* online learning (Richman et al., 2015).
	  • Avoid providing attention in response to problem behaviors as a result of compliance issues. This reinforcement continues to drive future problem behaviors *during* online learning (McGuinness, 2014).

Conclusion and Final Thoughts

From the moment this book became a thought, the struggle was to find the right title. There was never a doubt that the purpose of this book was to raise awareness for engaging and challenging gifted and advanced learners through online instruction. There was also no doubt that there are a multitude of books on the market about the latest and greatest tech tools, not to mention the endless supply of YouTube tutorials. While I have always been comfortable using technology in the classroom, I, too, found myself watching countless Bitmoji classroom tutorials and doing my best to adjust to full-time distance learning during the COVID-19 pandemic.

What I realized through much of my mandated trainings and personal drive to learn more about online and blended learning was that the main focus of available professional learning opportunities seemed to be on the "how-to" nuts and bolts of the tools and applications associated with online teaching, without ever hearing about how to use them purposefully and with integrity. Needless to say, there definitely was not a discussion about how they could be applied to address the needs of gifted and advanced learners. We need to think beyond how to "manage" technology in teaching and strive to also explore how technology can enhance, engage, and empower students in learning. This is a small nuance, yet a powerful one.

This brings me back to the title of this book. As you have read through the chapters, it is clear that this is neither a book focused on teaching the nuts and bolts of technology, nor a book on the latest technology tools and applications. Yes, that is important and needed. We cannot put the cart before the horse. However, it is my hope that this book fills a void in *how* to use those tools and applications to advocate for gifted education.

The goal of this book is to build capacity and understanding in how to integrate what we know about best practice in gifted education with online and blended learning. When the title focuses on *successful online learning* and *designing online and blended lessons* for gifted and advanced learners, it is focused on *leading* the instructional design with what we know is best practice in gifted education. When we, as gifted educators, are able to lead with strong gifted pedagogy and integrate *that* with innovative technology, we will have success. Technology without this foundation, can lack purpose and direction. While this book is just a snapshot of ideas, it is my hope that you were able to build a stronger foundation of how to better meet the needs of gifted and advanced students through online and blended learning.

While 2020 was definitely a year that will go down in history as being full of challenges, it also opened our minds to new possibilities, new solutions, and new innovations in learning and teaching. I challenge you to continue to learn, evolve, and grow in your instructional practice, and in doing so, advocate for the academic and affective needs of our gifted and advanced learners.

DOI: 10.4324/9781003238317-102

References

Allen, J. (2007). *Creating welcoming schools: A practical guide to home-school partnerships with diverse families.* Teachers College Press.

Bloom, B. (Ed.). (1956). *Taxonomy of educational objectives: The classification of educational goals. Handbook I: Cognitive domain.* Longmans Green.

Braunshausen, S. (2017). *What is the basal reading approach?* https://education.seattlepi.com/basal-reading-approach-1838.html

Brooks, R. (2010, October). The Mensa Hero Bracket challenge. *Mensa Bulletin, 539,* 34–45.

de Bono, E. (2016, [1989]). *Six thinking hats.* Penguin.

Donally, J. (2019). New realities. *Educational Leadership, 76*(5), 41–44.

DuFour, R., & DuFour, R. B. (2012). *Essentials for principals: The school leader's guide to professional learning communities at work.* Solution Tree Press.

Educational Endowment Foundation. (2020). *Remote learning: Rapid evidence assessment.* https://educationendowmentfoundation.org.uk/public/files/Publications/Covid-19_Resources/Remote_learning_evidence_review/Remote_Learning_Rapid_Evidence_Assessment.pdf

Fakolade, O., & Adeniyi, S. (2010). Efficacy of enrichment triad and self-direct models on academic achievement of gifted students in selected secondary schools in Nigeria. *International Journal of Special Education, 25*(1), 10–16.

Fredricks, J. A., Alfeld, C., & Eccles, J. (2010). Developing and fostering passion in academic and nonacademic domains. *Gifted Child Quarterly, 54*(1), 18–30. doi:10.1177/0016986209352683

Friend, M., & Cook, L. (2017). *Interactions: Collaboration skills for professionals* (8th ed.). Allyn & Bacon.

Gagné, F. (2008, May). Building gifts into talents: Brief overview of the DMGT 2.0. *Invited presentation at the Ninth Biennial Henry B. & Jocelyn Wallace National Research Symposium on Talent Development,* University of Iowa, Iowa City, Iowa.

Gentry, M., & Springer, P. (2002). Secondary student perceptions of their class activities regarding meaninglessness, challenge, choice, and appeal. *Journal of Secondary Gifted Education, 13,* 192–204.

Graham, C. R. (2006). Blended learning systems: Definition, current trends, and future directions. In C. J. Bonk & C. R. Graham (Eds.), *Handbook of blended learning: Global perspectives, local designs* (pp. 3–21). Pfeiffer.

Guilford, J. P. (1986). *Creative talents: Their nature, uses and development.* Bearly.

Houston Independent School District. (2020). COVID-19 response parent survey results, 2020-2012. *Research Educational Program Report.* Houston Independent School District.

Huang, Y., Backman, S. J., Backman, K. F., Mcguire, F. A., & Moore, D. (2019). An investigation of motivation and experience in virtual learning environments: A self-determination theory. *Education and Information Technologies, 24*(1), 591–611. 10.1007/s10639-018-9784-5

Juntune, J. (2013). *Differentiation of curriculum for gifted and talented students. TAGT OnDemand.* https://tagtondemand.com/product/differentiation-of-curriculum-and-instruction-for-the-gifted-and-talented-6-hour

Kahyaoglu, M. (2013). A comparison between gifted students and non-gifted students' learning styles and their motivation styles towards science learning. *Educational Research and Reviews, 8*(12), 890–896. doi:10.5897/ERR2013.1415

Kaplan, S. (2009). Layering differentiated curricula for the gifted and talented. In F. A. Karnes & S. M. Bean (Eds.), *Methods and materials for teaching the gifted* (3rd ed., pp. 107–156). Prufrock Press.

Lucas, M., Nelson, J., & Sims, D. (2020). *Schools' responses to Covid-19: Pupil engagement in Remote Learning.* https://www.nfer.ac.uk/media/4073/schools_responses_to_covid_19_pupil_engagement_in_learning.pdf

Madison, M. (2020, June 29). A parent guide: Support your child during virtual learning. *Edmentum.* https://www.edmentum.com/resources/brochures/parent-guide-support-your-child-during-virtual-learning

Martin, A. (2020). COVID notes from the field: Transitioning to digital learning. *Georgia Educational Researcher, 17*(2). doi:10.20429/ger.2020.170207

McCoach, D. B. (n.d.). *Goal valuation: Valuing the goals of school.* https://nrcgt.uconn.edu/underachievement_study/goal-valuation/gv_section0

McGuinness, C. (2014). *The effect of parent training on coping behavior in parents of children with developmental disorders.* Doctoral Dissertation Fischler School of Education Nova Southeastern University.

McGuinness, C. (2020). *Educating at a distance: A redistribution of roles.* [White paper]. https://files.eric.ed.gov/fulltext/ED605527.pdf

Mofield, E. (2019). *Curriculum, planning, and instruction for gifted learners [Conference session].* Kentucky Association for the Gifted Conference, Lexington, KY, United States.

Mofield, E., & Phelps, V. (2020). *Collaboration, coteaching, and coaching in gifted education: Sharing strategies to support gifted learners.* Prufrock Press.

Mofield, E., & Stambaugh, T. (2016). *Perspectives of power: ELA for gifted and advanced learners in grades 6–8.* Prufrock Press.

Mortera-Gutierrez, F. (2006). Faculty best practices using blended learning in e-learning and face-to-face instruction. *International Journal on E-Learning, 5*(3), 313–337. https://www.editlib.org/f/6079

Mullender-Wijnsma, M. J., Hartman, E., de Greeff J. W., Bosker, R. J., Doolaard, S., & Visscher, C. (2015). Improving academic performance of school-age children by physical activity in the classroom: 1-year program evaluation. *Journal of School Health, 85*(6), 365–371. https://www.wiley.com/WileyCDA

National Association for Gifted Children. (2019). *2019 pre-K–grade 12 gifted programming standards.* http://www.nagc.org/sites/default/files/standards/Intro%202019%20.Programming%20Standards.pdf

Neihart, M., Betts, G. (2020, March 21). *Revised profiles of the gifted and talented.* https://sciencetalenter.dk/sites/default/files/revised_profiles_of_the_gifted_and_talented_-_neihart_and_betts.pdf

Ng, W., & Nicholas, H. (2007). Conceptualizing the use of online technologies for gifted secondary students. *Roeper Review, 29,* 190–196.

Patrick, H., Gentry, M., Moss, J. D., & McIntosh, J. S. (2015). Understanding gifted and talented adolescents' motivation. In F. A. Dixon & S. M. Moon (Eds.), *The handbook of secondary gifted education* (2nd ed., pp.185–210). Prufrock Press.

Paul, R., & Elder, L. (2019). *Critical thinking: Tools for taking charge of your learning and your life* (3rd ed.). Pearson.

Phelps, V. (2021). Differentiation through independent study: The I-LEARN process. In A. Quinzio-Zafran & E. Wilkins (Eds.), *The new teacher's guide to overcoming common challenges: Curated advice from award winning teachers*. Routledge.

Phelps, V. (in press). Motivating gifted adolescents through the power of PIE: Preparedness, innovation, and effort. *Roeper Review*.

Powers, E. A. (2008, Summer). The use of independent study as a viable differentiation technique for gifted learners in the regular classroom. *Gifted Child Today, 31*(3), 57–65.

Rahman, M., Karim, R., & Byramjee, F. (2015). Prospect of distance learning. *Journal of Educational Research, 11*(3), 173–178.

Reddin, T., Cantu, M., & Carrington, A. (2017, February 19). *The padagogy wheel English V5*. https://designingoutcomes.com/english-speaking-world-v5-0/.

Renninger, K. A., & Hidi, S. (2011). Revisiting the conceptualization, measurement, and generation of interest. *Educational Psychologist, 46*(3), 168–184.

Richman, D. M., Barnard-Brak, L., & Grubb, L. (2015). Meta-analysis of noncontingent reinforcement effects on problem behavior. *Journal of Applied Behavior Analysis, 48*, 131–152.

Roberts, J. L., & Inman, T. F. (2015). *Assessing differentiated student products:A protocol for development and evaluation* (2nd ed.). Prufrock Press.

Robinson, A., Shore, B. M., & Enersen, D. L. (2007). *Best practices in gifted education: An evidence-based guide*. Prufrock Press.

Ronksley-Pavia, M., & Neumann, M. N. (2020). Conceptualising gifted student (dis) engagement through the lens of learner (re) engagement. *Education Sciences, 10*(274), 1–13. 10.3390/educsci10100274

Saeed, S., & Zyngier, D. (2012). How motivation influences student engagement: A qualitative case study. *Journal of Education and Learning, 1*(2), 252–267.

Siegle, D. (2019). Seeing is believing: Using virtual and augmented reality to enhance student learning. *Gifted Child Today, 42*(1), 46–52. 10.1177/1076217518804854

Stargardter, J. (2020). Virtual Instruction for Gifted Students. *National Association for Gifted Children*. https://www.nagc.org/virtual-instruction-gifted-students

Stein, S. J., Shephard, K., & Harris, I. (2011). Conceptions of e-learning and professional development for e-learning held by tertiary educators in New Zealand. *British Journal of Educational Technology, 42*(1), 145–165.

Swan, B., Coulombe-Quach, X., Huang, A., Godek, J., Becker, D., & Zhou, Y. (2015). Meeting the needs of gifted and talented students: Case study of a virtual learning lab in a rural middle school. *Journal of Advanced Academics, 26*(4), 294–319.

Taba, H., Durkin, M. C., Fraenkel, J. R., & NcNaughton, A. H. (1971). *A teacher's handbook to elementary social studies: An inductive approach* (2nd ed.). Addison-Wesley.

Torrance, E. P., Williams, S., & Torrance, J. P. (1977) *Handbook for training future problem solving teams*. University of Georgia.

Trna, J. (2014). IBSE and gifted students. *Science Education International, 25*(1), 19–28.

Vandenhouten, C., Gallagher-Lepak, S., & Ralston-Berg, P. (2014). Collaboration in e-learning: A study using the flexible e-learning framework. *Online Learning, 18*(3), n3.

VanTassel-Baska, J. (2009). *The integrated curriculum model. Systems and models for developing programs for the gifted & talented* (2nd ed.). USA: Creative Learning Press.

Webinar recap: Dr. Rhonda Bondie on scaling differentiation for blended learning. (2020, September 2). https://newsela.com/about/blog/dr-rhonda-bondie-scaling-differentiation-for-blended-learning/

Wigfield, A., & Eccles, J. S. (2002). *Development of achievement motivation*. Academic Press.

Wigfield, A., Tonks, S., & Eccles, J. S. (2004). Expectancy-value theory in cross-cultural perspective. In D. M. McInerney & S. Van Etten (Eds.), *Research on sociocultural influences on motivation and learning, volume 4: Big theories revisited* (pp. 165–198). Information Age Publishing.